easy Legal steps

...that are also
good for your soul

LISA FRALEY

To every entrepreneur and small business owner
who has courageously stepped outside of the box
to share a message that no longer can be contained.

To every lawyer who has created contracts and entities
to support business owners, without even knowing
how truly sacred such simple legal steps can be.

Contents

Welcome!...xi

A Loving Disclaimer xiii

Foreward xv

Introduction.. xix

Chapter 1. Website Disclaimer. Clarity. Root Chakra. 1

First Know What You Want...1

Beware of Murky Waters...2

How Legal Documents Give You Clarity 4

How Legal Documents Give Your Clients Clarity..............................5

When You Get Legally Covered, You Can Go Bare............................ 6

Your Legal Step: Website Disclaimer.. 8

The Purpose of a Website Disclaimer.. 8

Why You Shouldn't Cut and Paste 10

What Should Be Included?..11

Clarity and Website Disclaimers Align with the Root Chakra..........12

Root Chakra Mantra 14

Just Get Clear and Take Action 14

Start with Identifying Your Milestones 15

Encountering Stuckness 15

Our Ego Just Wants to Keep Us Safe (and Eating Marshmallows)........ 18

10 Ways Lack of Clarity Seeps into Your Business........................... 20

Give Yourself a Break and Pivot..21

Create an Opening for Clarity 23

What Happens Energetically When We Expand............................... 24

How I Got Clarity 26

What to Do When You Can't Find Clarity Anywhere....................... 30

3 Powerful Ways to Get Unblocked 30

Not Taking Action is Actually a Decision... 34

Key Takeaways from This Chapter.. 36

Now It's Your Turn …Legal Checklist & Business Self-Assessment........ 37

Legal Love™ Bonus Content:..38

Chapter 2. Client Agreement. Boundaries. Sacral Chakra. 39

Boundaries Can Feel Scary... 39

Legal Documents Create Practical and Energetic Boundaries................... 41

Why You Need Practical Boundaries... 42

Why You Want Energetic Boundaries 44

Identify Your Boundaries 45

Create Written Boundaries 48

Enforce Your Boundaries... 49

Are Electronic Signatures Allowed? 50

Your Legal Step: Your Client Agreement... 52

Client Agreements are Gifts 54

How to Feel Good Using Client Agreements... 56

Can't I Use One Contract for Everything?... 59

Don't Ever Guarantee Results 59

Boundaries and Client Agreements Align with the Sacral Chakra 61

Sacral Chakra Mantra... 62

Why is It So Freaking Hard to Set Firm Boundaries? 63

Being Compassionate Is a Good Thing (Except When It's Not) 64

Why We Let People Take Advantage of Our Kindness.................................. 65

Honey, My Boundary's Sprung a Leak 66

Key Takeaways from This Chapter.. 71

Now It's Your Turn ...Legal Checklist & Business Self-Assessment............. 71

Legal Love™ Bonus Content:.. 72

Chapter 3. Business Registration and Taxes. Confidence.
Solar Plexus Chakra. 73

Sleep-Depriving Fears and Worries... 75

What Does It Mean to be a Sole Proprietor?... 76

The Pros and Cons of Sole Proprietorship 77

Your Legal Step: Business Registration & Taxes... 78

When Should You Register Your Business and Deal with Taxes?.................. 79

Do I Have to Report My Income If I Only Have 3 Clients? 80

When Should I File a "Doing Business As" (DBA) Form? 83

Determine Where Your "Business Office" is Located 85

Confidence and Business Registration & Taxes Align with the Solar Plexus Chakra...**88**

Solar Plexus Chakra Mantra...**89**

The Gut is the Seat of Vulnerability..**89**

I Used to Be a Sugar Addict **91**

Your Body, Your Energy & Your Business (Psst! They're All Related).....................**93**

What if My Core Has a Muffin Top?...**95**

How to Feel Confident When You Don't Feel So Confident **96**

6 Simple Techniques to Feel Confident Now...**97**

Baby Steps That Don't Go as Planned **103**

Key Takeaways from This Chapter...**104**

Now It's Your Turn …Legal Checklist & Business Self-Assessment......................**105**

Legal Love™ Bonus Content:..**106**

Chapter 4. Website Terms & Conditions and Privacy Policy. Courage. Heart Chakra...**107**

My Favorite Church in the World...**107**

Courage Comes from the Heart..**108**

We're Rewarded When We Come From Service and Love, Not Fear.....................**109**

Lawyers and Entrepreneurs are Surprisingly Similar..**111**

Why Your Website is the Heart and Soul of Your Brand **113**

You Have the Right to Protect Your Work **114**

Legal Documents Don't Attract Lunatics or Lawsuits **115**

Your Legal Step: Website Terms and Conditions & Privacy Policy.........................**116**

Protect Your Content with Website Terms & Conditions...**117**

Protect Your Website Visitors' Info with a Privacy Policy **120**

Courage and Your Website Terms & Conditions and Privacy Policy Align with the Heart Chakra **122**

Heart Chakra Mantra..**122**

My Own Fear of Vulnerability and Visibility...**124**

The 4 Steps that Made Me Feel Safe to Film Videos **125**

Don't Try to Remove Fear: Just Go Around It...**128**

How to Find Your Courage When You're Really, Really Scared **129**

6 Steps for Taming Your Fear and Uncovering Your Hidden Courage................**130**

Courage (Like Crow Pose) Improves with Practice **131**

Why It's Worth the Risk...133

Key Takeaways from This Chapter..134

Now It's Your Turn …Legal Checklist & Business Self-Assessment........134

Legal Love™ Bonus Content:...135

Chapter 5. Terms of Use for Online Programs & Products.
Communication. Throat Chakra. 136

I'm the "Good Girl"..137

I Needed Permission..138

I Give You Permission..140

Your Legal Step: Terms of Use for Online Programs and Products..........141

Your Terms of Use are Your Sales Policies...141

Protect Your Income & Practically "Refund-Proof" What You Sell..........143

3 Big Reasons You Need Terms of Use...143

Do I Have to Use a Checkbox?..144

What Happens If Purchasers Don't Read Them?.......................................146

Longer Is Better..149

How to Handle Copycats and Swipers..150

Presume Innocence First..151

What to Do if Someone Swipes Your Stuff..153

We're Tested Before We Expand...155

Communication and Terms of Use Are Aligned with the Throat Chakra...........157

Throat Chakra Mantra...158

Declare It, Claim It, Own It..159

Show Up Fully Without Making Others Wrong..162

Losing Friends When You Speak Your Truth...165

Why We Can't Take Other People's Reactions Personally........................166

Key Takeaways from This Chapter..168

Now It's Your Turn …Legal Checklist & Business Self-Assessment........169

Legal Love™ Bonus Content:...170

Chapter 6. LLCs and S-Corps. Intuition. Third Eye Chakra. 171

Just the Facts, Ma'am...172

Law and Spirituality are Intimately Interconnected..................................172

That Time I Ignored My Own Intuition...174

How I Brought Law and Chakras Together 176

Your Legal Step: LLC or S-Corporation 179

6 Reasons to Go Pro with a Legal Business Entity 179

What the Heck are Assets?...179

A Little Disclaimer About Big Business Entities....................................183

The 3 Most Common Business Structures for Solo Business Owners.................183

Sole Proprietorship—The Simplest Way to Get Started......................183

Limited Liability Company—The Easy Business Structure 184

The Pros and Cons of an LLC 186

Can I Create an LLC Without Hiring a Lawyer?....................................188

Corporation—The Most Complex Business Entity.................................188

What's an S-Corp, Exactly?...189

The Pros and Cons of an S-Corp 191

Thank You, IRS!...192

When's the Right Time to "Go Pro" with an LLC or S-Corp?...................193

Which Type of Business Entity Is Right for You? 196

Intuition and Corporate Entities Align with the Third Eye Chakra 197

Third Eye Chakra Mantra 199

Our Intuition Is Always Talking to Us 199

10 Things We Might Not Want to Do After Tapping into Our Intuition.............. 200

Even When Your Hands Are Tied, You Still Have a Choice....................202

How to Access Your Intuition 203

Try This If You're Having Trouble Tapping In..205

Key Takeaways from This Chapter.. 206

Now It's Your Turn …Legal Checklist & Business Self-Assessment......................207

Legal Love™ Bonus Content:... 208

Chapter 7. Trademark. Leadership. Crown Chakra. 209

Stand as a Leader in Your Business..210

The Most Rewarding Charity Work I've Ever Done 210

That's Why They Say "It's Lonely at the Top" 213

You're Expected to Wear the Crown 215

It's Hard to Say No... 215

Legal Superpowers Give You Grace 216

It's the Policy of My Business..218

It's Time to Recognize Yourself as the Queen (or King)............................**219**

Ownership of Ideas and the Collective Consciousness............................**221**

You Can Fight Back Against Copycats and Swipers............................**223**

Your Legal Step: Trademark............................**224**

What Can You Trademark and Why Should You Do It?............................**225**

What About Copyright?............................**226**

Don't Let Someone Beat You to the Punch............................**228**

Step 1—The Trademark Search............................**229**

Step 2—The Trademark Application............................**231**

Oprah, an Entrepreneur, and a Trademark Walk into a Courtroom............................**233**

Own Your Power............................**235**

Is It Even Worth It to Trademark?............................**236**

Trademark is the Crown Jewel............................**237**

Leadership and Trademarks Align with the Crown Chakra............................**237**

Crown Chakra Mantra............................**238**

Key Takeaways from This Chapter............................**240**

Now It's Your Turn …Legal Checklist & Business Self-Assessment............................**240**

Legal Love™ Bonus Content:............................**241**

Going Forward............................**242**

3 Things I Want for You............................**245**

Congratulations!............................**246**

Legal Love™ Bonus Content............................**247**

Acknowledgments............................**249**

About the Author............................**257**

Endnotes............................**258**

Welcome!

Welcome! I'm so glad you're here to learn how to get legally covered to protect yourself, your business and your brand.

In addition to the easy legal steps and soul-centered principles in this book, here are even more ways to receive free legal tips, resources, legal templates and lots of Legal Love™ as you get your legal ducks in a row. I'd love to invite you to join my community!

1. **Join my Facebook tribe of Legal Lovers getting legally enlightened** at facebook.com/groups/getlegallyenlightened.

2. **Grab the Legal Love™ Bonus Content at the end of each chapter** to get free checklists, tips and assessments (over $1,300 value) – my gift to you!

3. **Get protected with easy-peasy legal templates, online courses, and one-on-one services** at lisafraley.com/services.

4. **Connect on social media** where you'll find more free legal tips and support:

Facebook	facebook.com/lisafraleylegalcoach
Instagram	LISA_FRALEY
Twitter	lisa_fraley
Pinterest	pinterest.com/Lfraley1

Linked In	lisafraley1
Google Plus	google.com/+LisaFraley1
E-mail	support@lisafraley.com

5. **Go behind the scenes to view my favorite books, business tools & self-care resources** at lisafraley.com/resources.

6. **Receive lots of love and support with business and life coaching services** at coaching.lisafraley.com.

Here's to getting legally covered!

With Legal Love,

A Loving Disclaimer

As a both a lawyer and a coach, it's important to remind you that the information provided in and through this book is intended to support you by making the legal steps and soul-centered coaching principles easy to understand, but you are responsible for how you apply them to your life and business.

This book is intended to be a guide for entrepreneurs and small business owners. It is not, nor should it be perceived or relied upon in any way as business, financial or legal advice. This book offers information of a general nature to help you understand legal and coaching concepts in a way that is easy, approachable, and fun.

This book is not intended to be a substitute for professional legal or financial advice that can be provided by your own accountant, lawyer, or financial advisor, nor does it, or should it be perceived to, create an attorney-client relationship between us. Throughout this book, you are advised to consult with your own accountant and lawyer for any and all questions and concerns you have pertaining to your own specific financial and/or legal situation. Laws vary from state to state and they are always changing; therefore, you want to work with your own attorney and accountant to be sure you are complying with up-to-date local, state and federal laws and regulations.

By reading this book, I am not responsible for your earnings, the success or failure of your business decisions, the increase or decrease of your finances or income level, your physical or mental health, or any other result of any kind that you may have as a result of information presented to you through this book. You are solely responsible for the application of any information obtained in or through this book and for your own results.

This book is not to be perceived as or relied upon in any way as medical advice or mental health advice. The information provided through this book is not intended to be a substitute for professional medical advice, diagnosis or treatment that can be provided by your own medical provider. Do not disregard professional medical advice or delay seeking professional advice because of information you have read in or through this book.

Throughout this book, the quotes and stories attributed to clients are fictional, but are based on real-life situations. Written permission has been obtained to share the identity of each real individual named in this book.

My intention as you read this book is that you move from feeling stuck and scared of the law to feeling confident and empowered so you can have the business and life you most desire.

Foreward

The law is really about love.

I remember the first time I heard Lisa say that. It was years ago. She was the keynote speaker at a conference I was also speaking at. And the way she spoke about the law—with such passion, such conviction—I could have sworn she was talking about discovering your life purpose or finding inner peace.

This wasn't the typical boring and confusing legal talk, filled with technical jargon and horror stories from worst-case scenarios. Instead, Lisa spoke about chakras and spiritual growth, about owning your power and stepping into abundance, about gaining clarity and sharing your gifts generously. Truthfully, it was about love. And seeing her up on that stage, so obviously in love with the work that she was sharing, it became clear to me that, like all things, the law is simply a container for love.

That talk must have clicked something inside of me. Because the day after we got home from the conference, I contacted Lisa to finally get my legal ducks in a row. Admittedly, at the time, I carried a lot of shame around the legal side of my business. I had grown a successful business over the few years since starting it. And there I was, a fellow featured speaker alongside Lisa, with honestly no idea if I was doing anything right—if the contracts I got from my coaching school actually protected me, or if I had registered my business correctly, or if I was at risk for getting sued.

I expected to be humiliated and overwhelmed during our work together. Instead, I felt safe and empowered and, most of all, really clear on exactly what I wanted to build. I felt like I had accessed this inner well of courage and security that I didn't even know I was missing. I felt like I could show up even more fully in my business—for myself and for my clients.

But what surprised me most about working with Lisa wasn't the fact that I was able to step into more security, clarity, and courage in my business; it was the fact that doing the legal work actually transformed my personal relationship.

At the time, my boyfriend Garrett and I had been dating for five years but still weren't engaged. I had been mentally planning to propose to him for years with this elaborate surprise trip to Italy. I knew that I was ready for our relationship to take the next step. But I kept convincing myself that we didn't have the time or money for the trip (my two favorite excuses).

Within a month of working with Lisa to officially form an LLC and get all of my legal protections in place, I had the sudden inspiration to go online and buy the tickets to Italy. I realized that some unconscious part of me was holding off on taking any steps toward marriage if Garrett's assets weren't protected from my business in case I ever got sued.

My legal protections literally gave me the security, courage, and expansiveness to marry the love of my life. They've allowed me to share my gifts from speaking stages to media interviews to luxury VIP days. They've supported me to confidently work with some of the top thought leaders in my industry. They've enabled me to feel supported to build a business and life I never in a million years would have thought possible.

Take it from a former skeptic: The law really is about love.

This book—this very book you hold in your hands—is a gold mine. I really mean that. There are millions of dollars and countless lives just waiting for you. And it's all on hold because of blocks you may not even be aware of right now. Everything you want is one the other side of your conscious and unconscious fears, blocks, and limiting beliefs.

In this paradigm-shifting book, Lisa does for the legal field what naturopaths and health coaches have done for healthcare. Rather than focusing solely on the "dis-eases" and legal problems when we're in the middle of a crisis, Lisa offers us proactive steps to get legally healthy. It's not sickness-care; it's healthcare. Legal healthcare. And Lisa shares a new way for us to relate to the law—using it to build the lives we want with clarity rather than defend against what we don't want. She coaches us to stop fearing legal dis-ease, and start stepping into *ease*. After all, as she reminds us so many times in this book, it's really about translating legalese into *legal ease*. So that we visionaries can get back to changing the world.

And it's no surprise that, in addition to being an attorney, Lisa is actually a health coach herself. She looks at the law and legal protections through a holistic lens, understanding the whole system and how it affects your chakras, your business, and your personal growth. Coaching us through this entire book. Cheering us on to be our best selves. Holding our hands and guiding us forward.

Easy Legal Steps is the game-changer heart-centered business owners have been waiting for. It's not hard to imagine some time in the not-so-distant future when we'll all become legal junkies—just as excited to protect our precious course or retreat as we are to get into the latest superfood. Wanting to get legally healthy rather than just interact with the law when there are problems. Unafraid to face our legal story and step into even more empowerment.

Where Lisa's brilliance shines most is in her understanding that everything is connected. Your legal protections affect your business successes affect your chakras and energy affect your entire life. And she helps us examine all of it so that we can bust through blocks, step up, play big, and become the people we want to be.

This book is an adventure, for sure. Through unconscious blocks, huge ah-ha moments, and massive uplevels. It's much more than just a book on the law; it's really a book about living a courageous, fulfilled life. The life you know you were born to live.

And, if you feel like you aren't living that life just yet—if you're wanting more clients or more money or the courage to speak on stages, work with your idols, or become the thought leader you were born to be—then Lisa has granted you the most generous gift possible. She has invited you into this revolutionary journey of clarity, security, empowerment, and love. To read this book is to forever fall in love with the law, your business, and yourself even deeper. After all, it's really about love. It's all about love.

Will you accept the invitation? Are you ready to see what's on the other side of those blocks? Are you ready to suddenly move forward in places you couldn't before?

Take a deep breath. Set your intention. And flip the page.

Prepare to be changed forever.

The adventure starts now.

-Mike Iamele

Mentor for Spiritual Entrepreneurs & Sacred Branding Coach & Author of *Enough Already: Create Success on Your Own Terms* (Conari Press 2015)

mikeiamele.com

Introduction

T hirty.

That's the age I was when I had what I call my quarter-life crisis, when I left the big cushy law firm.

Corporate America had squished my soul.

The lawyers at the law firm were whip-smart, and I had a few wonderful mentors (to whom I will be forever grateful), but overall I didn't feel that all parts of me were valued at the firm. My brain and work ethic, yes. My sunny personality, giggly laugh, and everything else that makes me unique – not as much. I don't mean to knock the firm. It was one of the top three law firms in the city, and I was honored to work in their health care and litigation departments.

It's just that the traditional large-firm mindset wasn't a match for my bubbly energy and style … but I didn't even realize it at the time. All I knew is that I lived on bags of peanut M&Ms and coffee and about five hours of sleep a night—and, like a lot of Corporate America, that made me a stressed-out, exhausted mess.

When I left the firm, I went straight to therapy.

I took four months to regroup. I did the projects I hadn't had time for before, like cleaning out closets and taking trips to Paris and Las Vegas. I reassessed what I wanted to be "when I grew up." My dad suggested reaching out to his friend who was a life coach. I did, and I ended up becoming a life coach myself.

I never would have guessed.

Fast forward a decade.

A perpetual student, I enrolled in the Institute for Integrative Nutrition and added "health coach" to my resume. As a health coach, I worked one-on-one with clients and I gave 72 corporate wellness seminars in 18 months, teaching employees how to make banana smoothies, avoid the "dirty dozen" pesticide-laden fruits and veggies, and swap out cans of Coke for glasses of lemon water.

My health coach friends who knew I had been a health care attorney kept asking me what they needed to do to protect their health coaching businesses. At first I resisted diving back into the law, but soon my own business coach was encouraging me to "bring all of my gifts together" to help coaches and entrepreneurs get legally covered to protect their programs and courses. I embraced my legal past and I combined my caring coaching approach with my health care legal skills to become a Legal Coach® and Attorney.

Fact: Most people hate lawyers. And the law.

They think that lawyers are cold, corporate, and unapproachable. Not going to lie; some lawyers can be a bit salty.

So many clients have told me that they were afraid to approach their family's long-time lawyer or a local law firm, because they thought that lawyers would be unwelcoming and unapproachable. They were intimidated to walk into a law office and were worried they wouldn't understand archaic words or they'd feel stupid asking questions. They told me that they've been scared to get on the phone with a lawyer because they will be charged hundreds of dollars just to ask a few questions.

But lawyers, and the law, don't have to be scary.

If you've been afraid of the law or had a bad experience with a lawyer, you're not alone. Maybe legal documents have felt overwhelming, intimidating, and boring. Maybe the legal parts of your business are the last thing you want to deal with. Maybe you would never set foot in a law office. Maybe you haven't found a lawyer who gets you and your business and who can teach you about the law in plain English.

Lucky for you, that's exactly why I have written this book. To turn legalese into *legal ease.*

The way I see it, legal documents are like green smoothies for your business. They boost the health and strength of your business on the front end so everything runs smoothly on the back end. They fill your business up with vitamins and nutrients from the start, so you don't end up needing catastrophic legal care in an unexpected crisis.

Legal documents can give you strong and supportive language to limit your liability and protect your income, brand and business–and also written with "Legal Love™." They don't have to be cold or scary at all.

As an entrepreneur or small business owner, you're allowed to protect your business and keep it safe —without turning into a pit bull—or fearing your clients will think you're unapproachable when you send them a legal contract to sign (I promise.).

You can get your legal ducks in a row to boost your credibility, raise your professionalism, and strengthen your boundaries, without being ferociously harsh, attracting negative energy, or feeding a scarcity mindset.

And since I'm an attorney AND a holistic health and life coach, I've brought together key legal steps to support and protect your business with important coaching concepts.

Why? Because I approach everything holistically.

That's why I call myself a Holistic Lawyer® (and even trademarked the term.)

I've brought all parts of myself together and use my coaching lingo and spiritual concepts to teach why doing things legally right keeps you from later having to put up a fight.

So many coaches, entrepreneurs, and business owners like that I've brought my bubbly, "perky" cheerleader personality and high-energy nature to the serious profession of law to make it more accessible, approachable, and affordable—and WAY more fun. They love that I add color and graphics to legal templates rather than use boring black and white paperwork (quite unheard of for a lawyer.)

And, they love that I look at business holistically and make a connection between the law and the chakras and explain why you need legal protection in a way that is easy to understand.

It's important as a business owner to be legally enlightened because if you aren't aware how your legal documents protect you, you won't feel confident using them, and you'll keep yourself small, stuck, and exposed. When you're small, stuck, and exposed, you can't make more money or help more people.

You can only take steps forward to make more money and help more people if you get yourself unstuck, and one of the best ways to get unstuck is to unpack the areas that are holding you back.

How do you do that?

This book will teach you seven legal steps that protect you in practical and energetic ways and seven chakra-aligned principles for growing a business that have helped me move through my own fears.

I'll share why both the legal steps *and* the principles matter when you want to catapult your business forward.

Not only does the law provide critical tools to protect yourself, but when you take legal steps, you strengthen your boundaries, plug energy leaks and raise your energetic frequency. Unlike most lawyers, I believe that "the law is spiritual too" and these unexpected energetic results are what I call the "spiritual side effect of the law." I've seen time and again that when you protect your business in practical ways, you boost your business in energetic ways too.

You may think I'm crazy for saying that the law is spiritual or that legal documents can be full of "Legal Love™", that's okay. I don't blame you. Believe it or not, I thought it was crazy too at one time. It sounded so out there (even to me) that for a long time, I didn't talk about the spiritual side of the law at all—not a peep, not a word. For two years.

No other lawyer that I've ever known has spoken about the law as spiritual or uttered "Legal" and "Love" in the same breath—and I've never been one to rock the boat.

But this belief in me grew and grew, and it got to the point where I knew that it was unavoidable. I couldn't stay quiet. My intuition was screaming at me. I had to start owning what I knew to be true and add more spirituality into how I talk about law, even though it scared the bejeebies out of me. It's now one of the core beliefs that I teach.

When you take legal steps, you shift your vibe to attract more of what you want.

But, it goes even farther than that.

After helping hundreds of entrepreneurs use legal templates, create business entities, and file for registered trademarks, it dawned on me one day when I was sitting at my desk working on my laptop that there are seven legal steps most entrepreneurs take in a certain order as your business grows, and these steps align with the seven chakras and seven key soul-centered business principles.

Bingo.

This revelation was such a gift, both for me as a lawyer and for all heart-centered business owners and entrepreneurs who want to have strong legal documents that are also good for your soul.

You'll see how when you combine legal steps with chakra-aligned principles, you can move you from stagnant, stuck and scared of the law to confident and empowered as a business owner —and with a thriving six- or seven-figure business to boot!

In the coming chapters, you'll learn how each legal step, each principle, and each chakra connects to support a thriving, heart-centered business and how they cover your buns. You'll learn how easy it is to take these steps, one step at a time, as you expand your work.

You'll see examples that I share about real clients who took these legal steps and shifted their businesses in enormous ways. You'll see how they felt safer, more secure, more confident, and more empowered to play bigger. You'll see how they received more of what they wanted, attracted more clients, made substantially more money, and stopped playing small. You'll see how their entire energy, life, and business changed exactly as they had hoped it would.

My unique approach to the law and business can save you time, money, worry and angst with easy legal tools that you can implement in far less time than taking a bazillion online courses or figuring it out on your own.

You're welcome to read the book straight through or jump around based on the legal step you need (like a Website Disclaimer or Client Agreement), the principle you want to enhance (like confidence or courage), or the chakra you want to support (like the root chakra or crown chakra).

Each chapter contains information about a legal step, a principle and a chakra. Here's a quick guide to what's inside:

- If you're launching your first website or need more clarity in your business...

    Chapter 1 shows you how to get base layer website protection with a Website Disclaimer, find more clarity, and align with the root chakra.

- If you work with one-on-one with clients and wonder how to protect yourself or you want stronger boundaries in life or business....

Chapter 2 shows you how to protect your income from one-on-one clients with a Client Agreement, create better boundaries, and align with the sacral chakra.

- If you want to set your business up right as a Sole Proprietor or you're seeking more confidence as a business owner...

  Chapter 3 shows you how to get set up properly as a Sole Proprietor with Business Registration & Taxes, find more confidence, and align with the solar plexus chakra.

- If you want to protect your website content from Swipers and Copycats or you're feeling scared and want to be more courageous...

  Chapter 4 shows you how to protect your website & build trust with your Website Terms & Conditions and Privacy Policy, dig deep to find your courage, and align with the heart chakra.

- If you offer group programs, online courses, or digital products and need legal terms, or you find yourself holding yourself back from expressing your true voice or message...

  Chapter 5 shows you how to protect your course content with Terms of Use for Online Programs & Products, focus on clearer communication, and align with the throat chakra.

- If you're wondering if you need an LLC or S-Corp or you're feeling blocked in your intuition...

  Chapter 6 shows you how to know when it's time to form an LLC or S-Corp, tap into your intuition, and align with the third eye chakra.

- If you're curious about Trademarking and have no idea where to begin or you want to feel like a leader in your own business...

  Chapter 7 shows you whether Trademarking is the right step for you, step into leadership as the queen/king of your business, and align with the crown chakra.

And, if you have no idea where to begin with the legal steps for your biz, no worries! Just start at the beginning and read straight through to the end.

It's that simple.

When you follow these legal steps and chakra-aligned principles, both law and business will feel more approachable, safer, and easier to understand.

Based on the hundreds of clients I've helped, and on my own personal journey as a lawyer and entrepreneur, you'll see how these steps can get you to the life and income you want much faster...and, most importantly, in a way that is soulfully aligned.

Just one thing you need to know before you dive in: This book is not designed to substitute for working with your own attorney or accountant, but rather to serve as a guide so you can learn about basic legal steps and concepts in a way that is easy to understand. It is not legal advice for you specifically, since each situation may vary and the law may change at any time. This book is designed to give you an overview of seven legal steps at high altitude; it's not intended to be heavy in legal principles, case law or statutory citations that could feel overwhelming. There are legal treatises and textbooks that can give you that level of depth. And while you can take legal and financial steps solely on your own, it's highly recommended to work with an appropriate attorney and accountant to support your business as you grow.

Here's the bottom line: When you get your legal documents in place and allow these soul-centered principles to help you go from stuck to empowered, you can move forward and create the business you really want.

Each legal step and principle is a critical ingredient in the recipe for success. Each step is a crucial part of the whole. There's no need to put all of the steps in place at once— just go one step at a time to use your resources wisely and not get overwhelmed.

This book will help you do it with ease and grace using easy legal steps…that are also good for your soul.

Join me as we navigate through each legal step, each principle, and each chakra together.

Congratulations for stepping up to take legal steps to support your business, to move from scared to strong, and to boost your energetic vibe to create the life and business that you most deeply want.

You're already on your way!

With Legal Love™,

Lisa

Chapter 1.

Website Disclaimer. Clarity. Root Chakra.

I f there's one thing that every entrepreneur needs—and doesn't often have—it's clarity. Clarity is critical at every stage of your business.

It's simple really: When we're clear, we take action, attract clients, make money, and serve the world. When we're unclear, we don't.

As an entrepreneur or small business owner, you already know there's no one giving you assignments, telling you exactly what to do, or handing you a paycheck every week like at a day job. There's no financial security—no bonus, no pension plan, no 401(k) that has your back. There's just you and your business, so to make the income you need to support yourself, you have to take action.

But to take action, you need clarity first.

Clarity is the first step to success. You have to know what you want and how to get there so you know where to direct your time and energy. It takes a clear path ahead.

First Know What You Want

Having clarity creates safety. Because when you feel clear, you feel safe to take action, to put yourself out there and to step outside of your comfort zone. If you don't feel safe, you don't move forward and you stay stuck.

When we're vulnerable or uncertain, we just want to hide behind a large piece of furniture, maybe forever. We certainly don't want to be visible or seen or heard when we aren't clear about our message, who we're here to serve, or our truest purpose on the planet.

We need clarity about the how, the what, and the when. We need to know HOW we want to feel, WHAT we want to accomplish, and WHEN to take the next step so that we can achieve and receive what we most desire.

We need to feel safe and secure before we can do anything else – or we'll remain stuck in the muck, right where we are.

If you're feeling unclear and you can't move forward in your business, you might hear yourself saying things like:

- "I'm overwhelmed by what step to take first."

- "I'm feeling vulnerable—I have no idea how to protect myself and my business."

- "I worry about getting sued."

- "I'm afraid I could be putting myself and my family at risk."

Don't worry, these are normal fears. As you keep reading, you'll learn how to shift these feelings to be more confident and secure because you'll know how to protect yourself, and you'll learn the right legal and business steps to take.

Beware of Murky Waters

Not surprisingly, when you don't have clarity, things can look murky.

Think about a pool of murky water. Murky water is stagnant, cloudy, and often really, really stinky.

The water may look dark brown or even black from dirt that has been stirred up from the bottom. It might smell like your teenage son's dirty socks or like a compost pail that hasn't been emptied in a while. If you're like me, you'll wonder if there are slimy worms below the surface or a frog that could jump up and startle you.

You have no idea what's underneath the surface, and you certainly aren't going to stick your finger in the muck to find out. You can't see even a glimmer of your reflection looking back at you. You feel tensed for what might jump out at you or focused on how you might protect yourself if something leaps out and catches you off guard.

Although you can't see it clearly, prior experience tells you there's a lot of gunk in that water. You decide it's better to avoid it altogether, and you walk away.

In contrast, now think about a clear pool of water. I can almost hear you breathing a sigh of relief and feel your energy lighten because now you can totally see what lies beneath. You can peer down and see wisps of your hair, your sparkling eyes, and your wide smile reflected back to you. You trust that what you see is real and clear ... and you feel safe.

You can tell there're no scary critters in that pool of water, and you're confident that there's nothing to be afraid of. You can see to the bottom and don't have to waste your energy feeling timid or frightened.

It's a simple analogy, but it's the same for business. So often we feel stuck looking at that murky water—or business confusion—when all we want is a nice pool of cool, clear water that reflects back to us exactly what to do next.

You can have clarity in your life and business, even when you aren't sure where to find it—or how to get it.

Your first step as an entrepreneur or small business owner is to get clear so you can act from a calm, empowered place—rather than staying in a fear-based state, not knowing what kind of danger may pop up out of the muck and startle you.

First, let's talk law, then we'll talk business. Since I'm a Legal Coach® and Attorney, we'll start with the legal step, but because I am also a Holistic Health & Life Coach, we'll also talk about the equally important business side, including how to get clarity when you don't seem to have it.

Legally speaking, one of best ways to create clarity for yourself and others is to put a base layer of protection in place so you feel grounded and safe that your business buns aren't legally naked or exposed. Getting clear about your policies is key to having a thriving business.

You may be surprised to know that taking legal steps gives you tremendous clarity.

When you take legal steps, two significant things happen:

- YOU receive clarity.

- OTHERS receive clarity.

Believe it or not, the process itself of putting legal documents in place for your business creates clarity. Why? Because you need to know what your policies are, where you draw your lines, and where your own boundaries are before you can put them into a written legal document to hand to a client or post on your website.

How Legal Documents Give You Clarity

This might sound obvious, but before you create any legal document outlining your policies and boundaries, you need to be clear about them yourself. It's just like how you need to have gas in your car before you drive to your neighborhood coffeehouse. You can't get your mocha almond milk latte without making sure your gas tank isn't on empty.

Sitting down to use a legal template or have a legal document created for you is the same. Before you create the document, you need to think through your expectations and limitations about your policies for key areas of your business, including:

- How you want to offer services

- How you like to communicate

- How and when payment works

- How missed appointments are made up or forfeited

- How you draw legal liability lines

- How you resolve conflict disputes

When you're unclear about your policies and you don't have them in writing, you end up with people swiping your content, asking for refunds, or refusing to pay you…and you don't have a written policy with strong legal language to fall back on.

But, when you create legal containers like contracts and terms to hold and support your business, you define how you want show up for your clients when you work together, and how you expect your clients to show up for you, and you have fewer legal messes.

The clarity you gain by thinking through your options and deciding where you draw your lines allows you to shift from uncertainty to feeling safe and secure with peace of mind–all because your legal policies are all spelled out in writing.

How Legal Documents Give Your Clients Clarity

Not only do you get clear when you put your policies in writing, but you give your clients, website visitors, or other partners the gift of clarity too.

1. **Others know your policies**, what your expectations are, and how you want them to show up in your relationship. This level of detail and foresight around what happens if a client misses a call or is late with a payment creates fewer communication misunderstandings and allows you to enjoy a smoother relationship.

2. **Others get better results** because when they know from the start what is expected of them, they can provide services or come to your calls or appointments more focused, committed and eager to work for the results they want through your work together.

3. **Others relax** because they know up front what your policies are which can reduce ambiguity or confusion in your relationship and prevent sticky issues from arising.

When your clients, website visitors and partners have better outcomes and experiences, it results in better testimonials and recommendations for you, which can easily translate into more income, more clients, and more ease in your business.

Simply put, legal tools can help you go from chaos and confusion to clarity and confidence.

When you are clear, others are clear. Everyone wins.

When You Get Legally Covered, You Can Go Bare

It's easy to write off the legal parts of your business as not important, or to say that you aren't ready for them yet. You may think your business is too small, or you don't have the money.

But whether you are a brand new or a seasoned entrepreneur, taking legal steps gives you clarity, safety, security and a feeling of being grounded—and you can't put a price on peace of mind.

You can avoid the inner angst and gnawing fear that a client's going to freak out one day and come after you. Or that a disgruntled client is going to say nasty things on social media and shine a huge floodlight on your biz while you stand there naked with no legal protection to cover you.

When you protect yourself from the "crazies" (as my mother would say), you expand and grow, rather than stay stuck and small, exactly where you are.

When you get legally covered, you can go bare.

You feel safe enough to vulnerably shed your fears, to share your truest, deepest, most heartfelt work with the world—which, ultimately, is what you are here on this planet to do.

Of course, you don't ever want to be so vulnerable that you feel stark naked, but you do want to bare your heart and soul to the world through your love and service to others, and you can do that more confidently knowing you have a strong legal foundation under your feet supporting you from the ground up.

This is EXACTLY why I named my legal course "get legally covered so you can go bare" and why I have written this book. I want you to feel safe and secure with the right legal protections in place so you can "bare" your heart and soul to the world without fear, doubt, or worry.

I know from working with hundreds of clients that it's difficult to move forward to create new programs if you are worried about the legal parts of your business. It's hard to promote your discovery calls to attract new clients. It's no surprise your message keeps changing and you aren't comfortable putting yourself out there.

Having a lack of clarity is painful. It's scary. It's uncomfortable. It's time to stop the pain.

To grow your business, you need to step out of your comfort zone, launch new programs and services, take more risks, and show more of who you really are. You can do this more easily and comfortably when you know your legal documents have your back.

Your Legal Step: Website Disclaimer

These days most entrepreneurs and business owners have a website. If you want to operate your business in the online world, you're going to have at least a site, even if it's a very basic one.

Most people share information about their background, expertise, and products and services on their website.

You also may want to have a blog, articles, quizzes or information on your site, and the last thing you want to worry about is that someone reading your latest blog post on the benefits of kale starts eating boatloads of it without checking with their doctor—even though they're on blood thinners and should avoid kale altogether.

If you have a website, your Website Disclaimer is your first step to protecting yourself. It's the most basic level of legal protection.

Even if your website isn't fancy or big or you just have nothing more than landing page or a one-page site, you'll want to be sure you have a solid Website Disclaimer in place that covers the basics so you are clear and intentional about where you draw your lines.

The Purpose of a Website Disclaimer

The purpose of your Website Disclaimer is to let people know what you DO—and DON'T do—as a small business owner or entrepreneur so they don't get confused and come after you. It's linked through the footer of your website, so it is visible from every page of your site with ease.

The two main reasons to have a Website Disclaimer are:

1. **To disclaim your liability** so that people don't blame you if they misapply information that you shared on your site or—heaven forbid—sue you. You want to give and share information on your site without worrying that someone will come after you. You need to be clear that you're not legally responsible for the actions your website visitors take after reading something included in a blog post, article, or video.

2. **To empower your website visitors to take responsibility** for their own lives and businesses. You want to tell them that you are providing information on your site to help them become better informed and educated but they need to use their own judgment before applying what you say to their own life or situation.

For example, you don't want to be blamed for not specifying that website visitors should check with their doctor before they use any recipes or suggestions on your site. After all, you can't be standing over their shoulder when they're making a kale salad that they shouldn't be eating because they're on blood thinners, right? Right. Your Website Disclaimer will tell your website visitors to talk to their own medical, legal, financial and other licensed professionals before implementing any information that's provided on or through your website.

The purpose of a Website Disclaimer is to empower you to draw your lines around liability, and to inform every website visitor to use care and judgment when applying any of the info on your site to their own life or business.

And, even if your website visitors don't even read your Website Disclaimer, they are still bound by them. They still must follow them. They are implicitly agreeing to them when they land on your site and start surfing around. That's good news for you. Because if there's ever a conflict, your

Website Disclaimer is proof that you set the intention and clearly outlined your policies for the use of your website relating to liability.

Bottom line: Your Website Disclaimer is designed to be super-clear about where your liability stops and where your website visitors' responsibility begins.

Why You Shouldn't Cut and Paste

Your Website Disclaimer needs to be robust and personalized for your business—because your training, expertise, niche and programs are not like anyone else's. You want to make sure that your document is thoroughly covering what you do and the unique way you do it.

Generic cut-and-paste documents designed for everyone don't fully cover you because they may not take into consideration the exact type of work that you do as an online entrepreneur or bricks-and-mortar business owner, and they may not contain language that supports your specific training or licensure.

And while it can be tempting to copy and paste the Website Disclaimer of someone else who is in your same industry, you don't want to do that for three big reasons:

1. **It could be a violation.** Unbeknownst to you, copying a friend's document is actually taking (some might say stealing) work that someone else paid for and you may be violating their copyright. Even if you are given permission by your friend to use it, it may result in your friend violating the purchase terms from their lawyer which could land them in trouble, so you don't want to put them in that position.

2. **It may not even fully cover you.** The language your friend used may not be fully appropriate for you. If they cut and pasted language from the internet, or used someone else's language, they may not have had legal assistance in creating the document, so you both

could end up using legal language that doesn't even sufficiently cover either of you in the work that you do.

3. **It's bad karma.** It may feel like a quick fix to get some legal language up on your site, but in the long run, that karmic debt will hang over you and come back around in a spiritual sense which you don't want. Copying someone else's work probably isn't truly in alignment with your core values and it's bad karma.

You're wise to invest in your own Website Disclaimer that you can personalize and place on your site, and know how exactly it protects you.

What Should Be Included?

You may be wondering what exactly needs to be included in a Website Disclaimer. There are a few important sections that you'll want to include that draw your lines around liability.

Take my client Sarah, for example. Sarah is a health coach who lives in Texas and works with one-on-one clients to help them to live a Paleo lifestyle. Sarah came to me because she was nervous about making food or supplement recommendations in blog posts because she didn't want someone to cut out food groups like grains and legumes who really needed them in their diet for whatever reason.

Sarah was worried and wanted to make sure she had a Website Disclaimer that made it clear she wasn't giving medical advice and that people still needed to talk with their doctor before implementing any of the recommendations on her site.

In Sarah's case, it was particularly important that her Website Disclaimer not only included language stating that the information on her site was just educational and informational, but she specifically needed thorough language stating that she wasn't a doctor or medical professional and she wasn't giving medical advice through her site. She also had a number of testimonials on her site and she recommends products and affiliates in her blog posts and articles.

A good Website Disclaimer is a few pages long and is linked through the footer of your website. It's not just a few sentences at the bottom of your home page (I call that a "mini-Disclaimer".)

Sarah needed a robust, thorough Website Disclaimer that had clear language spelling out that: (1) she is not holding herself out as a medical practitioner, registered dietician or licensed nutritionist, (2) her website is not substituting for the advice that can be provided by a medical practitioner, (3) she is not providing medical, therapeutic, religious, legal, accounting or financial advice through her site, (4) she's just providing education and information, (5) her testimonials are just examples, (6) any product recommendations or affiliate mentions throughout her site are just suggestions, (7) visitors are personally responsible for implementing any suggestions on her site – and much more.

Each small business owner or entrepreneur is going to have slightly different language or sections in your Website Disclaimer based on what you need to explain and disclaim, so you may or may not need the same sections Sarah needed. (This is a perfect example as to why copying someone else's document really isn't ideal.) It's important that you include the right language for your type of work and expertise.

(If you want to know 6 core sections that should be in EVERY Website Disclaimer, grab the Legal Love™ Bonus Content at the end of this chapter.)

Clarity and Website Disclaimers Align with the Root Chakra

As I shared in the Introduction, each principle in this book is aligned with a legal step and with one of the seven main chakras, the energy centers of the body.

I associate the Website Disclaimer with the root chakra because it helps you feel safe, secure, and grounded, especially when you are just starting out with a new website.

The root chakra is our lowest chakra of the seven main chakras. The Sanskrit word for this chakra is *Mooladhara*. "*Mool*" means root, and "*Adhara*" means support or base. In the body, the root chakra encompasses the base of the spine, the lower lumbar vertebrae, and the pelvis.

This chakra is represented by the color red, and it has been associated with being connected to the earth, our place in our tribe, and feeling grounded, stable, secure and safe.

When you first launch your website or you do a website rebrand, you can feel vulnerable. You can feel exposed and scared, wondering if people are going to like the site you worked so hard to build, and wondering if you are somehow unknowingly exposing yourself to risk.

When you put your Website Disclaimer in place, you are taking the initial step to creating a grounded legal foundation for your business. You give yourself security and safety that you have some legal language in place to fall back on if needed. This causes a noticeable energetic shift in the way you feel. You feel more clear, more confident and more secure because you have drawn lines around your liability and taken a first step to legally protect yourself.

Having legal clarity helps you stand on solid ground so you can go forward and expand your business. Just as the Website Disclaimer is a key legal step to take, clarity is an essential element for grounding you as an entrepreneur.

On some days, clarity is tricky though. If you struggle to find clarity on any given day, you may want to take a moment to pause and center yourself with this Root Chakra Mantra:

Root Chakra Mantra

When you are seeking more clarity, security and safety
in your life or business,
you can set your positive intention with this Root Chakra mantra:

"I am clear. I am safe. I am secure. I am grounded."

Just as it's important to get clear about using legal policies like a Website Disclaimer, it's important to get clear on the business side as well. Clarity is a theme that will emerge over and over to refine and redefine as you grow and expand your business.

We've talked law, so now let's talk business.

Just Get Clear and Take Action

It sounds obvious, right? You hear it all the time: "Just get clear and then take action, and you'll be successful."

It's a true statement, for sure ... but not so fast. It's easy to say: "Just get clear about what you want and then go after it." It's another thing actually to *do* it.

Why? Because as a business owner, clarity is needed at so many levels. You need to see your big picture, your larger business goals and milestones, and then you need clarity with each smaller step that's needed to reach those milestones.

Making so many decisions at so many levels can feel overwhelming, so what do you do if you aren't feeling so clear?

The easiest place to start is with your big targets.

Start with Identifying Your Milestones

Milestones can be easily measured in business, so they're a great place to begin. For example, you can set goals for yourself that feel good to you, like:

- "I'm brand new, so I just want to secure my first client."

- "I'm starting out and I'd love to have a $5,000 month."

- "I'm offering a new course, and I'm holding the vision for a 6-figure launch."

- "I'm going to break the $1 million mark this year."

What are your milestones for your business? What do you hope to accomplish that feels really big this year – or even this month? Don't worry about how big it is to someone else or how it might actually happen, but take a moment to define your big goals. You may want to grab a journal and jot them down right now.

Encountering Stuckness

Even after you've identified a few milestones, you might still find yourself stopped in your tracks because the steps to reach the milestones — well, they can be much harder to figure out. You may not know exactly what steps to take, or when to take them, to reach your goals, and indecision can grind you to a halt.

Take my client Margaret, for example.

Margaret was a life coach who had been in business for about eight months. She had identified a milestone as having a six-figure business this year. She was already working with one-on-one clients to help them make more time for self-care in their lives and romantic candlelight dinners with their sweeties, and she had made about $45,000 to date. She was ready

15

to expand her income streams, but she wasn't sure if she wanted to focus next on having workshops and overnight retreats or whether she wanted to create online courses. As a result, she had been completely paralyzed for the past few months. She could do both, of course, over time, but she didn't have the time, money, or mental headspace to create both revenue streams at the same time and still work with her current clients. She was emotionally torn because she didn't know which to create first—retreats or courses?

Margaret loved the idea of inviting people to experience a high-end retreat. She envisioned the oceanfront beach resort where she would hold it. She could picture her guests immersed in luxurious self-care, squishing white sand between their toes as they sat in circle and journaled about their deepest desires, ate fresh organic fruit and veggies, and unwound in peaceful meditation classes. When she thought of offering retreats, she felt expansiveness and lightness in her energy, and she was excited.

But Margaret also wanted the freedom and flexibility to work from home in her yoga pants and pink fuzzy slippers. She loved the idea of wearing no makeup and loosely pulling her hair up in a ponytail so she could just hunker down and create an online course on her laptop. She liked the idea of creating a course that she could offer over and over as an evergreen course. When she thought about offering online courses, she felt financial relief and security, and that allowed her to relax.

Both options felt good. Margaret felt torn between an expansive, immersive, tactile experience for herself and her clients, and the security and comfort of a home-based online course offering.

While Margaret had a clear big-picture image of both options, she felt stuck. She didn't know where to begin in finding the ideal resort location for a high-end, high-cost event. She also didn't have an online course delivery system set up, and she was intimidated by the technology side of her business. While she could see the outcomes for both options clearly, she felt like she was looking into big pools of murky water when it came to taking action. She didn't know which to do first and she didn't want to make a mistake. She'd been in limbo for months, and she'd done nothing.

When she contacted me, she candidly shared that she felt like deciding to offer the retreats would betray the other part of her that wanted herself and her clients to have the experience of an online course. I could tell that she had high standards and didn't want to make the wrong decision, screw it up, or waste her time or money.

As is often the case with my clients, talking with Margaret allowed me to bring my holistic health and life coaching skills forward to help her step back, assess her business options, and offer emotional support and guidance.

I reflected to Margaret where she had clarity: She knew she wanted to both offer retreats *and* create online courses. She was clear about the options that would bring her the most joy and boost her bank account, and that level of clarity was important at the macro level.

But when she went a bit deeper to the micro level, her desires were mired in stuckness, and her indecision about what to do next was draining her finances, energy, and time.

Margaret had no boss standing over her telling her what to do or making decisions for her. She had no roadmap, no GPS, no coaching program that would tell her which direction was the right one for her. She could talk with her soul sisters and biz buddies, and she could be guided and coached, but she alone had to make the final decision about what was right for her and her business.

There's certainly freedom in being our own boss and decision-maker, as all entrepreneurs know, but that very freedom can be what makes entrepreneurship challenging. You feel you need to figure it all out for yourself. You feel the burden of bringing in your own income. You feel overwhelmed, paralyzed, exhausted, and uncertain as you consider the many directions you can take your business.

And when we're in a space like Margaret was, trying to decide between two options that are equally enticing, it's easy to feel overwhelmed and do nothing.

When we're paralyzed, we don't move forward. When we're exhausted, we don't feel motivated. When we're uncertain, we don't take action.

Consciously, we want clarity. We want to know what to do, how to do it, and what steps to take. We don't like staying stuck, resisting money, or withholding our gifts from the world. The whole reason we got into business in the first place was to help people and support ourselves. But when we don't have the right tools, tips, or timing, no wonder it's so easy to stay in a place of inaction.

Clarity can feel so evasive at times.

But you know what?

Lack of clarity is just Fear's way of being sneaky.

I am convinced that confusion is just Fear's little trick to keep us stuck and safe.

Our Ego Just Wants to Keep Us Safe (and Eating Marshmallows)

The job of the Ego is to keep us safe and alive, so instead of giving us clarity, it keeps us unclear so that we don't have to put ourselves at risk or step up in new ways that feel terrifying.

The Ego wants to keep us right where we are at this moment because it knows we're alive right now. This sometimes means that it wants us to stay small, squished down, and uncertain so that we stay alive at all costs. Ego tries to keep us safe by keeping us in a state of Fear.

And, boy, can Fear take over your usually sharp mind and fill it with uncertainty! The next thing you know, you're sitting in Margaret's shoes gnawing your fingernails as you ponder which direction to take your business, or you're watching the pile of bills stack up on your desk with no clear path to generate the income to pay them off. You walk around with a sick feeling in the pit of your stomach. It feels icky. It feels scary. It feels frustrating, not to mention exhausting and damaging, to be without any clear answers.

A lot of entrepreneurs find themselves camped out in indecision for long periods of time. It's like their Ego has pitched a tent, built a fire, told Fear to grab the marshmallows, and sat down to roast s'mores. The Ego has zero sense of urgency to pack up the tent, tell Fear to take a hike, leave the cozy campsite, and head home.

But, all camping analogies aside, there's one thing I know for sure. You can't stay in stuckness for long if you want to have a successful business. You've got to get the Ego on board so it can snarf down its toasted marsh-mallows, roll up the sleeping bag, pack up the car, and get back to business.

If you're not paying attention, lack of clarity can sneak up on you and take over. Sometimes you don't even know it is happening until it's too late.

Fear and lack of clarity show up wearing so many disguises.

Fear isn't always obvious. It uses trickery and costumes—like a wolf in sheep's clothing—to appear to be anything but Fear.

Fear can show up in our minds and conversations sounding perfectly rational. We pay attention to what sounds like logic, never realizing that it's filling our mind with rubbish. I know at times I have found myself believing Fear's whispers and shouts. I've ended up stuck and small and squished, yet feeling wise and smart because I think that I'm heeding some important warning.

But it's all a trick! Here are ten ways that I've identified that lack of clarity shows up to keep you stuck. See if Fear has snuck into your business in any of these ways:

10 Ways Lack of Clarity Seeps into Your Business

1. **Mental Blocks.** You have no idea what your next new program should be, who your ideal client is, or what your website text should say. You're experiencing a mental block and you can't break through it.

2. **Imposter Syndrome.** You know you aren't walking your talk and you feel like a complete fraud, so how could you possibly give anyone else advice ... and why would anyone listen to what you have to say?

3. **Perfectionitis.** You worry that if you don't look or sound perfect, or if your course materials don't look just right, no one will want what you create and you'll let everyone down. You'll feel that you're a failure.

4. **Inner Critic.** You beat yourself up that "it's not good enough" and you're afraid that it—and you—will be berated about your lack of ability, skill, knowledge, design, content, and anything else you think it's up to par.

5. **Comparisonitis.** You find yourself stalking your idols on social media and comparing yourself to them saying you "should" be where they are, which leaves you feeling like you are "behind" or your work is "less than" theirs in some critical way.

6. **Analysis Paralysis.** Your smarty-pants rational mind analyzes the heck out of different options and you can't make a decision because there are pros and cons for every option—and you don't want to make the wrong choice.

7. **Shame Games.** You feel embarrassed that your website looks out of date or your online course, program, or e-book isn't well designed or beautiful enough, and you're afraid people will think that you're not professional enough or can't be taken seriously.

8. **Shoulding on Yourself.** You "should" all over yourself by telling yourself you "should" be doing this or you "should" be doing that because everyone else is doing it, and if you don't do it, people will think you're not cool and they won't buy your stuff.

9. **Not Knowing Enough.** You worry that despite investing thousands of dollars in dozens of courses and coaches, you don't have enough training, knowledge, or experience for people to hire you and get the results they're seeking.

10. **Technology Twisters.** You let technology issues stump you and stop you, rather than reaching out for tech help to set up your sales funnel or your opt-in sequence for your next launch or biz offering.

Whew. That's some list. See, I told you Fear could be sneaky.

Give Yourself a Break and Pivot

Isn't it time to give yourself a break?

Isn't it time to be gentle with yourself, recognize your strengths, honor your unique gifts, and give yourself some freedom and ease from the shaming and blaming and "shoulding" all over yourself? Isn't it time to pivot?

It's time to liberate yourself from a whole laundry list of nasties and make a few shifts to say goodbye to:

- **Comparison.** Remember that your truth and gifts are unique and not like anyone else's—and the world needs to hear what you have to say.

- **Shame.** Remember that you are exactly where you are supposed to be, and where you are right now is perfect and divinely timed to unfold exactly as it should.

- **Guilt.** Remember that if you feel you haven't done enough or learned enough, trust that you know exactly what you need to know to help someone who isn't as far along in their journey as you are.

- **Stress.** Remember that a little self-care and self-gentleness can go a long way when you are working hard to build the business and life that you want. Find small pockets of time to work out, take a bath, meditate, soak in a hot tub, take a walk, watch a mindless TV show, or do whatever fills you up to alleviate stress for a while.

- **Shoulds.** Remember that there are no "shoulds" when it comes to owning your own business. You get to choose which path is right for you. Your journey will not be exactly like anyone else's. Do what feels right for you—and only you; your clients will sense you're speaking, writing, and acting in alignment and automatically be drawn to you.

Take a moment to remind yourself of the clarity, confidence and power you already have when you turn off the Ego's determined rants and raves. Turning down the volume on the Fear and turning it up on the empowerment is what will break you free from the indecision.

I don't know about you, but I am tired of the "shoulds," the shame, the guilt, the stress, and most of all, the comparisonitis. It's exhausting. And unnecessary. It feels so much better to make business and life decisions that feel good, bright, free, expansive, empowered, authentic, and true to yourself, don't you agree?

Can you take a moment to get rid of the "shoulds" and the comparisonitis and give yourself the freedom and expansiveness to let your business unfold exactly as it should, trusting that what you are doing is good enough, that who you are is good enough, and that your work is good enough to help improve someone else's life?

I want you to remember the knowledge, experience, generosity, service and desire that is present within you right now and let it give you the fuel to define clear actions to move forward in your life and business.

Create an Opening for Clarity

When we tap into our sense of freedom, expansiveness, and "enoughness," we feel a lightness in our energy that translates into our work, expanding well beyond our website, latest offerings, e-newsletters, programs, products and services. Remembering our "enoughness" creates an energetic opening. An opening for clarity.

When we shift our internal energy from stuck and stressed to free and empowered, we create space for clarity.

Let's go back to Margaret for a second. Remember how Margaret had clarity around her big-picture goals? Remember how she knew she wanted to create a feel-good, life-changing physical experience at a beachfront resort by offering retreats and also wanted the ease of creating an impactful online course from the comfort of her own home? Even though she couldn't decide which one to create, she could see two clear options.

Through our conversation, Margaret realized that both options made her feel excited and relaxed inside—and when she realized she really couldn't go wrong with either option, she took a huge, soul-deep sigh of relief. She shifted internally to a feeling of expansiveness and openness, instead of feeling contracted and stuck for the first time in months.

All I did was help her step back and look at what she already knew she wanted—an impactful experience for her clients, financial security, and ease. Her shift to a feeling of expansiveness based on what she already knew to be true on the inside showed up on the outside as well, which you'll hear more about in a bit.

Bottom line: When we release ourselves from Fear's clutches and give ourselves permission to shift to a place of expansiveness, we create an opening for clarity that moves us forward.

What Happens Energetically When We Expand

Let's take a minute to dive deeper into what happens when we energetically and emotionally expand like Margaret did—and how that translates into more clients and money.

We already know that when we take legal steps that help us get clear, we shift to feeling more grounded and safe. We've talked about how when we feel grounded and safe, we expand to feel open and free, and we move away from feeling stuck and small. When we stop and acknowledge anything that we're already clear about, we create an environment that invites MORE clarity about our next steps, even if we don't know what they are just yet.

Just by shifting to a feeling of expansiveness, opportunities suddenly appear. It sounds crazy, but it's probably happened to you. Many times.

Like when Margaret decided to browse social media and saw a link to a blog post about how to run a high-end overnight retreat. Or a friend mentioned to her how much she loves the customer service she gets from her online course platform delivery system. Or a client tells Margaret about a recent VIP retreat she attended. Nuggets of information and guidance showed up for her without having to do anything to search for them.

Think that's just a coincidence?

I don't think so.

My spiritual mentor and sacred branding coach, Mike Iamele, says that when we tune into our internal energy and get into a space of expansiveness, it's the ENERGY that people are drawn to, not the specific words on a website or the images on a sales page that we've been anguishing over.

People are drawn to how they FEEL when they experience us embodying alignment in our energy. Its positive undercurrent flows through our words and business and draws people to us.

When we're aligned with our values and what we know to be true, people are drawn to what we're offering—whether it's a high-end retreat at an exotic resort or an online course crafted while in yoga pants and fuzzy slippers.

Sure, it's great to have a cool website and savvy sales pages, but that's not really what draws people in. They may catch someone's eye, but that client won't sign up with you if they don't feel an emotional and energetic connection to your energy that comes through on your website or sales page.

It's not solely about the words or the marketing strategies we use in our business —it's about the energy *behind* the words.

Not only that, but when we're open and free and expansive on the inside, on an energetic level, it opens a clear channel to the Universe to know what to bring to you.

Expansiveness is a high-vibration energetic state that creates an opening and lightness without the obstructions, resistance or blocks that prevent what you want from reaching you. When you're stuck or unclear, you can't emit that level of energetic frequency and people can sense your tentativeness in your energy.

This may sound totally theoretical, and it is certainly "woo woo," so let me give you a specific example from my own life.

How I Got Clarity

After I graduated from the Institute for Integrative Nutrition (IIN), I offered health and life coaching services and corporate wellness trainings as a health coach. I had started coaching my peer health coaches while we were in IIN together because they knew that I had become a life coach back in 2003 through Coach U, the oldest coaching school in the country.[1]

My health coach friends knew that I'd worked as a health care attorney in a large corporate law firm working with hospitals and physicians, and they kept asking me for help on the legal front.

I told them that while there are a ton of great traditional attorneys out there (including many of my dear friends from law school), I would bet that most aren't familiar with health coaching, online courses, or virtual cleanses, and I encouraged them to find an attorney who understood their line of business.

That's when my health coach friends and clients started turning to *me* for help. They said, "But, Lisa, you're an attorney who is also a health and life coach and you totally understand what coaching is without us even needing to tell you!" It was true—I knew what opt-ins, Ontraport, and online shopping carts were. I had an insider's understanding of the coaching business.

They were right.

At first, I experienced a ton of inner resistance because there were few, if any, other lawyers who were trained as health coaches and life coaches and who were combining their gifts to work with online business owners. There was no blueprint to follow. There were no cookie cutter programs to tell me how to do it. There were few examples of other lawyers who were working in the online space, and of the one or two I could find, I knew I wanted to do it with more love infused into the law and less harshness and "cover your ass" attitude—which is how I came up with "Legal Love™" as my tagline.

I wanted to combine the caring of a coach with the leadership of a lawyer, but it was so far outside the box from the traditional practice of law. WAY outside of the box. My vision to infuse love and coaching into the law was unique. It was unexpected and unprecedented.

When I first hung up my shingle as a Legal Coach®, I was lit up inside. I was excited. I was passionate. I was aligned. But I didn't have a Legal Coaching® website. I didn't have any sales pages. I didn't do social media ads. I didn't even have an e-mail distribution list (and didn't for about two years!) or send out e-newsletters. I offered free 20-minute Legal Chats to anyone who signed up. That's it. That's all I did. I made sure that people knew that I wasn't giving state-specific legal advice or formally representing them, but that I was giving them tools and education as to the general legal steps needed to protect and support an online business in general.

And guess what happened? I had gazillions of Legal Chats, created simple legal templates and online courses, filled each person up with so much Legal Love™, and helped them gain clarity that my business grew simply by word of mouth.

Clients felt my heart, my passion, and my genuine desire to help them feel safe, secure, confident and empowered in their business by taking the right legal steps at the right time.

They were terrified of traditional attorneys and what they thought were intimidating, stuffy law firms that charged too much and left them confused and unsure whether what they had purchased even covered them. Even if the lawyers had done a fantastic job (which I am sure most did), they didn't feel emotionally supported, confident or empowered when they walked out the door, which was disconcerting for the clients.

Because of my training as a coach, I knew that how clients felt after working together was just as important as the legal documents they received.

Other life coaches, business coaches, and online entrepreneurs came to me and referred clients to me because my focus was on teaching what

27

legal steps are important early in business generally, and what could wait, so they could spend their hard-earned dollars wisely in the best ways to protect their income, content, and brands.[2]

Yet, while working my full-time job, my part-time coaching income grew from $1,200 a month to $2,500 a month to $4,000 then $5,000 then $7,500 then $9,000. I knew that if I could consistently make $7,500-9,000 per month working part-time as a Legal Coach®, I could easily make over six figures working full time, so that's when I knew it was time to leave my day job.

Now, a few years later, my list is many thousands and my gross income is multiple six-figures from my do-it-yourself legal templates, online legal courses, and relationships with other attorneys.

I share these details with you because when I created my Legal Coaching business, I had no clarity. I had no plan. I started out taking just a few simple actions that felt energetically aligned and expansive, and I offered free information, direction, value and love, and then created DIY legal templates, packages and courses.

The feedback that I received was that people could feel my warmth. They could tell that I cared. They sensed my genuine interest in their story and their business and my blonde hair and perky personality defied many stereotypes about lawyers. I didn't charge by the hour. I didn't take retainers. I didn't engage in adversarial work.

My "come from" was to approach entrepreneurs and small business owners with the love of a coach with a strong spiritual side and the knowledge of a lawyer who makes the law easy, accessible, colorful, and relatable by aligning seven key legal steps with the seven main chakras.

My clients connected to my energy, and they could sense I was aligned—and they were drawn to that.

But it took me a long time to get clarity myself. I had to wade through some murky water.

It would have been easy for me to get caught up not knowing how to blaze my own trail. It would have been easy to stay small and uncertain about how to build a business by adding a new spiritual twist to the law. I took baby steps, painfully and cautiously, with boatloads of coaches, spiritual healers, and soul sisters by my side and I figured it out one day at a time.

Just as I identified the seven legal steps that align with the seven chakras, I discovered seven soul-centered principles that I wish I had known from the start. I'm sharing the very shortcuts and tips that I used so you can save the time, angst, worry and stress. Think of them as a pair of tall rubber boots to wear to get through the murky water.

It would have been easy to have not brought together my gifts of being a coach AND a lawyer to help you take legal steps to support your business and protect your income, content, and brand.

But that wouldn't have served you well. You would still have your head in the sand, scared to talk with an attorney. You would still be struggling to find a lawyer who truly understands your work. You would have continued to ignore taking the legal steps needed to feel grounded, protected, and expansive—and that would have left you frustrated, stressed, and exposed.

By staying small and unclear, I would have deprived thousands of business owners of the gift of feeling safe, secure, confident and empowered.

The same is true for you and your gifts.

If you stay small and safe, who is being deprived right now of your knowledge, gifts, insights, support, and love?

If you stay stuck or unclear—like Margaret—how many people are being denied the experience of a lifetime in a high-end retreat or receiving the exact information they need from an online course to take their next big step in business?

Don't deprive people from benefitting from what you uniquely have to offer.

What to Do When You Can't Find Clarity Anywhere

You might be saying, "Okay, I get that expansiveness creates clarity which creates clients which creates money. Great. But what do I do when I feel aligned and expansive on the inside but I still can't seem to find clarity about what steps to take next? What then?"

There are many ways to find clarity, and what works may vary somewhat from person to person. But there are three ways that I have found to consistently create clarity, both for my clients and for me.

You'll notice that I said "consistently CREATE clarity." Yep, that's right. We create clarity. It's not something that just happens TO us, even when we're feeling expansive. Expansiveness is just part of the equation. Clarity is something that is created BY us.

3 Powerful Ways to Get Unblocked

I'm sharing three ways to get clarity because there's nothing that I hate more than coaches or books that tell you WHAT to do, but not actually HOW to do it. I wanted to be sure to give you tools not only that take you from stuck and scared of the law to confident and empowered as a business owner, but the business principles that are the keys to success too.

Here are three of the best ways I've found to create clarity:

1. **Clarity comes through surrendering to how things are right now.**

Surrendering to accept a situation for what it is "right now" can remove resistance, struggling, tension, and anxiety. When you humbly stop fighting against your circumstances and acknowledge them for what they are in this precise moment, you relax. Your energy changes.

By the way, "right now" doesn't mean "forever." It doesn't even mean "tomorrow" or "next week." It just means surrendering "right now", in this moment of time, today.

It's my belief that what's happening in our lives "right now" is a direct result of the past decisions that we've made. What's happening now reflects our past mindset, wishes, dreams, desires, wants, and goals. We set those intentions last year, last month, last week, or even yesterday, but it can take some time for them to show up in the present.

Some manifestations are instantaneous, but other manifestations take longer.

Take weight loss, for example. Besides being a lawyer, health coach, and life coach, I've also been certified as a fitness instructor. (I know, I have many interests. I am a Gemini, after all!) From my studies to become a personal trainer, I know that you can eat 1,600 calories a day and work out for one hour a day and it can still take a good six weeks before you see a reduction in body fat, increased muscle mass, or more than a few pounds of weight loss show up on the scale.

This can feel frustrating when you are eating well and exercising and you want to see instantaneous results. But, the body doesn't work that way.

The weight we weigh today is a direct result of decisions we made yesterday, last week, last month, and last year.

The body needs time to catch up. That's why fitness experts always say "weight loss takes time."

On the other hand, take the example of finding a great parking space. Results can be instantaneous.

The last time you went to the store, you may have been trying to find a good parking spot and ended up driving around and around the block thinking "Geez! I never find a good parking space"—and sure enough, you never found a good parking space. You had to park rows and rows away from the restaurant or store entrance and then hoof it to the door.

But once you shift your energy and your mindset to truly believe that "A parking space always opens up for me just when I need it," and you drop the resistance to "what is," sure enough, you'll find that a parking spot often opens up for you right when you need it.

Manifestation of a parking space can happen instantly when you make the internal shift from a state of disbelief and resistance to a state of belief and openness.

Funny how that works.

When we remove resistance that may be expressed through our emotions, thoughts, energy and awareness, the answers come more freely. We lose the weight without trying. We find perfect parking spots more often. We attract our ideal clients. We build our next course or program with ease. We have so many clients that we need to start a waiting list.

When we drop the frustration about how things are, we create the space to open to new beliefs about ourselves and the world and parking spaces. Our energy becomes unblocked of old stories, outdated beliefs, outgrown habits, and outlived concerns.

When we surrender to the present moment and to the way things are now—even if we would far prefer to be having a different, more positive experience—we create space for clarity to come through.

Sometimes, even by creating a little silence in our busy, always-wired days, we can quiet the mind to practice presence and surrender to what's happening in this moment. We can engage in activities like exercise, meditation, yoga, drinking a hot cup of tea, snuggling on the couch with our sweetie, spending time with our kids or pets, or doing whatever helps us slow down and create new space to gain presence.

For me, running, snuggling, and meditating change my mindset and energy instantaneously for the better. These simple activities calm me so that I can open and shift to a different energetic state.

When we stop using our energy to wish that things were different and instead surrender in the present moment to what is, we stop creating resistance. We stop pushing against life, which frees us up to shift our energy and mindset to focus on the future.

It feels like an oxymoron to surrender to the present to get clarity about the future, but somehow it works like magic.

2. Clarity comes through making a decision and taking action.

The second way to create clarity is to decide and act.

Yeah, I know—you're probably thinking "But, Lisa, don't I need clarity first BEFORE I make a decision? How do I make a decision if I am not clear about what decision to make?"

Ah, there's that beloved Ego showing up again trying to protect you. I told you that Ego was sneaky.

Don't get me wrong; our Ego does many things to keep us safe and we need our Ego to keep us protected from life-threatening situations or serious harm. (Thank you, Ego!) However, the Ego isn't always discerning as to the type of danger that could hurt us or what is merely taking us out of our comfort zone a bit. The Ego senses it ALL as danger and triggers questions like these to try to keep us safe and sound, right where we are at this moment. The Ego's intentions are good, but its tactics are terrible.

Back to Margaret. Remember how she couldn't decide whether to offer luxurious high-end retreats or simple online courses that she created from home while wearing her yoga pants and fuzzy slippers? She got clear about wanting to do both, but her state of confusion was just her Ego trying to keep her safe.

By keeping Margaret in limbo, her Ego kept her from taking a risk that felt scary and WAY outside her comfort zone. She didn't have clarity about which direction to go, so she didn't have to decide which option to choose.

33

And while it may appear that she wasn't making a decision or taking any action ... underneath the surface, she actually was. By staying in indecision, Margaret was making a decision.

She was deciding not to take action.

That's a decision.

Not Taking Action is Actually a Decision

Not taking action is actually a decision. Wrap your mind around that for a moment.

Margaret did have clarity about what she really wanted to do, even though she thought she didn't. She constantly weighed the options, looked at the pros and cons of each, and she anguished over what to do. She wanted to choose one over the other ... but by not taking a risk, selecting one and diving into tasks needed to bring one to life, she stayed stuck.

She—or at least her Ego—was clear that the action she should take to move her business forward was to stay stuck and take NO action.

Staying stuck was her decision.

Before anything else would change, Margaret had to own that she was making a choice to stay exactly where she was. She had to surrender to her reality and not fight against it. When she realized that her current state was based on the decisions she had made in the past, she realized she could make a shift for the future.

By owning her choice to maintain the status quo, Margaret dropped her resistance and created an opening for clarity. When we talked through it, she realized that her resistance sneakily showed up as Perfectionitis, Analysis Paralysis, and Technology Twisters. Once she had clarity about the source of her resistance, she could address each of those blocks and dismantle the specific worries that had kept her stuck.

She'd been so focused on whether high-end retreats versus online courses made the most sense for her time and money that she hadn't looked inward to figure out the underlying reasons for her decision to remain in indecision. Until she was ready to do that, nothing would shift for her.

To recap:

- Recognize that when you're in a state of frustration or fear, it's just the Ego trying to keep you safe.

- Understand that indecision is just an illusion of a decision that you've already made.

- Acknowledge that there doesn't need to be judgment around feeling fear or staying stuck.

Recognizing your decision for what it is—even if it's the decision to do nothing differently than what you do now—gives you clarity. It removes resistance and frees you up to assess whether that decision is still the right choice for you, or you're ready to go in a different direction. Accepting the decision you've made allows you to begin to unravel it and address the underlying worries so you can move forward with clear action.

3. Clarity comes through getting support.

When you surrender to the present, recognize the decisions you've made, and move toward taking action, you may find yourself feeling uncomfortable. When you decide to branch out in new ways and walk foot-first into that murky water, you can feel vulnerable.

That's why every coach out there—including me—will tell you that you shouldn't take action alone. When you're stretching yourself and your business in new ways, it's best to have support from a coach or a mentor who is farther along in their business to help you identify your goals, hold a bigger vision, and keep you accountable to taking action.

Why is that so critical?

Because nothing changes if you don't change.

Let me repeat that: Nothing changes if you don't change.

Changing your circumstances, mindset, goals, and actions is more challenging without someone supporting you and cheering you on.

As I often tell my own clients, you can do ANYTHING with courage and support.

Whether you take gigantic leaps forward or tiny baby steps to grow your business doesn't matter. There's no right or wrong way to become successful.

There's no one-size-fits-all business plan. There's no timeline other than a divine plan co-created by you and the Universe (or whatever higher power you believe in). There's no perfect way to create a course or offer a program or create a sales page. There are many ways, and that can make it harder. Sometimes, the greater the options, the harder it is to choose.

You want someone by your side to help you surrender to the present, make decisions, take actions and stretch you just a bit further forward. You want someone who will honor your fears but at the same time remind you that you can be scared and take inspired action anyway.

That's exactly what a coach does. A coach helps you get clarity.

Key Takeaways from This Chapter

Clarity is key to having the business and life that you most deeply desire. If you're feeling lost or unclear, putting your legal documents in place, like your Website Disclaimer for your website, can help you get clear. We all peer into murky water sometimes; the key is to get clear as soon as possible so you can keep moving forward and taking action. Use the tips from this chapter to help you take the first steps.

Your first legal step is a Website Disclaimer.

Your first soul-centered principle is clarity.

Your first chakra is your root chakra.

Now It's Your Turn …

Use this Legal Checklist and Business Self-Assessment to help you uncover resistance, walk through the murky water (wearing your tall rubber boots!), and get clear about your business decisions and legal steps so you can move forward taking clear action.

Legal Checklist:

1. Do you have a website?

2. Do you hold yourself back because you worry someone might come after you?

3. Are you feeling exposed or naked without legal language to protect you?

4. Do you have clarity for your website visitors about your basic legal policies?

5. Do you have your Website Disclaimer up on your site? (If so, congratulations! You get a gold star!)

Business Self-Assessment:

1. Do you feel clear about big goals and milestones?

2. Do you see a clear pool or murky water ahead of you right now?

3. Do you experience any of the Top 10 Ways lack of clarity sneaks into your business? Which ones resonate most with you?

4. Have you created an opening for clarity? How does the feeling of expansiveness show up in your body? Do you feel more relaxed? More optimistic? More ease-filled?

5. Which of the 3 Powerful Ways to Get Clarity will help you most if you're feeling blocked? Which one sounds the most appealing to you?

Don't forget to grab your Legal Love™ Bonus Content!

Legal Love™ Bonus Content:

"6 Key Sections that Should Be in Every Website Disclaimer"
Free download at lisafraley.com/disclaimerkeysections ($197 value)

Chapter 2.

Client Agreement. Boundaries. Sacral Chakra.

Boundaries are critically important for having a successful business. A boundary is an edge. A limit. A point of demarcation. A border. A perimeter. A frame.

Merriam-Webster Dictionary[3] defines a "boundary" as:

- Something (such as a river, a fence, or an imaginary line) that shows where an area ends and another area begins

- A point or limit that indicates where two things become different

- Unofficial rules about what should not be done

- Limits that define acceptable behavior

- Something that indicates or fixes a limit or extent

- Something that points out or shows a limit or end

- A dividing line

Boundaries Can Feel Scary

I don't know about you, but to many people, boundaries can feel harsh. They can feel unkind. They can feel cold, corporate, rigid, and

39

uncomfortable. They can represent so many qualities which you don't want to have.

But *not* having boundaries can be even scarier.

As a business owner, it can be super-easy to continually share extensive time, money, and energy from your own coffers because you're trying to be kind, polite, supportive and generous to others.

Think about it—how often have you heard yourself or another entrepreneur saying something like this?

"I have a one-on-one client who never pays me on time. Just the other day, a second client asked for a refund and she's halfway through my program. All I want is to do is help people and get paid without chasing money or giving refunds. Is that really too much to ask?!"

Late payments and missed payments. One of the worst feelings when you don't get promptly paid for your hard work.

So many entrepreneurs who work with one-on-one clients find themselves chasing down money. They worry and stress due to money woes because their clients:

- Make late payments—or they don't pay at all.

- Ask for refunds—halfway through the program.

- Miss calls or sessions—wasting their time and yours.

- Or blame you for not getting results they want—though it's not really your fault at all!

Check out these real-life scenarios told to me by different types of clients. Have you dealt with these or similar situations in your business?

If you're a Health Coach:

"A client will not stop texting me. She texts at night and on weekends and wants me to tell her what vitamins are in this kind of vegetable or how much protein is in quinoa and beans. My contract says I am only available from 8 am–5 pm but I still get texts from her and I feel like I have to reply to her at night or on the weekends."

If you're a Spiritual Healer:

"All of my clients will always pay me. I have good energy and all of my current clients pay me on time. I don't want to attract negative energy to me, so if I haven't had any payment problems, why do I need to use a Client Agreement or to put anything in writing?"

If you're a Business Coach:

"I'm scared to use a written agreement because I'm afraid I will come off as cold and corporate and my clients will run the other direction. I'm trying to build a warm, caring relationship with them, and the last thing I want to do is shove a harsh legal document at them reminding them of Corporate America. It feels yucky."

If you're a Website Designer:

"I have a Client Agreement that I've used for about a year, but I never enforce it because it's scary to hold my clients to it. I worry that they will quit and not make their final payment after I create their website, or tell their friends not to work with me because I'm not very flexible."

What can these business owners—and you—do about it?

First, we'll address handling boundaries through your legal documents, and then we'll talk about ways to create better boundaries in business.

Legal Documents Create Practical and Energetic Boundaries

It's my core belief that the law is both practical and spiritual. It may sound odd to hear a lawyer say that, but, as I've shared, I believe that legal documents support you in two ways—practically and energetically.

What I mean by that is, when you put legal documents in place, you are creating boundaries on two different planes—both as "practical boundaries" and what I call "energetic boundaries."

Legal documents help you create practical boundaries on a material level to protect yourself, your biz, and your brand. Strong legal language delineates your rights and protects you and your business. Legal documents safeguard your work in practical ways, protect your intellectual property, and defend your integrity, and you can fall back on them in court if necessary.

Taking legal steps in your business for practical reasons is paramount. Contracts, agreements, trademarks, and legal terms are all great examples of practical boundaries set forth in writing to give you security, safety, peace of mind and protection.

Why You Need Practical Boundaries

You tighten your boundaries on a practical level when you use these legal protections:

- **Client Agreements** with one-on-one clients protect your income and time, with your policies for payments, refunds, and missed calls all spelled out in advance.

- **Contracts** with team members like your website designer, graphic designer, and virtual assistant help everyone operate from the same understanding of who does what task.

- **Terms of Use** for your online courses, group programs, and downloadable products give you legal language to fall back on if someone copies your stuff. (Terms of Use are discussed in Chapter 5.)

- **Trademarks** protect your original and creative taglines, business name and more. (Trademarks are covered in Chapter 7.)

The other type of boundaries are what I call "energetic boundaries," and they're not typically addressed by most traditional lawyers. Just to clarify, "energetic boundaries" don't have anything to do with faith or religion;

it's simply a term that I use to distinguish boundaries formed on an energetic or spiritual level from boundaries created on a material level.

Let me explain.

Legal documents and contracts can help you create energetic boundaries to create containers, borders, and lines of demarcation on an energetic level. They can help you keep AWAY what you don't want to draw towards you (like people who swipe your copy or duplicate your program guide without obtaining permission) and bring TOWARD you things that you want (like ideal clients, more income, and greater freedom).

Energetic boundaries aren't boundaries that are written on paper or apparent to the eye, but they're often powerful undercurrents happening below what appears on the surface.

If your energetic boundaries have leaks based on underlying beliefs, old stories, and energetic blocks, it can manifest in people not respecting your practical boundaries by asking for refunds or missing calls or stealing your work. When your energetic boundaries are strong and solid, you attract situations that almost magically fall into your lap with ease – like dream clients, exciting opportunities, unexpected gifts, and flowing streams of income.

When you shore up your energetic boundaries, you plug those slow, drippy faucet-like energy leaks that are zapping your time, vibe and money—sometimes while you aren't even fully aware of it.

By taking legal steps, you strengthen your energetic boundaries because you are creating clear lines and expectations about how you want to be treated which makes you more inclined to attract people who respect boundaries themselves. Like attracts like, so the clearer you get about your boundaries, the more you attract people who like clear boundaries too, and the less likely you are to attract what you don't want.

Why You Want Energetic Boundaries

When you tighten your boundaries on an energetic level, you:

- **Plug money leaks** so you attract clients who pay you on time and request fewer refunds, allowing you to keep more income.

- **Protect your time and knowledge** so you don't draw in those late-night-and-weekend chronic texters or people who only want info from you for free.

- **Keep away** clients who drain your time, energy, and attention so you have more time for your ideal clients who respect and value your time and expertise.

- **Attract more** of what you want—more money, more clients, more freedom, and more luxury.

When you use written legal documents and agreements, you automatically uplevel yourself and strengthen your practical boundaries and energetic boundaries. Everything shifts for the better.

For example, take my client Kate who is a relationship coach. When Kate started using a Client Agreement that drew clear boundaries about when clients miss a call with her, she noticed that clients stopped canceling at the last minute or missing their calls altogether. She felt her own energy shift to a position of strength and power, and she noticed her clients seemed to behave more professionally and respectfully towards her, and didn't cancel on her anymore.

By putting her Client Agreement in place and getting clear about what she would and wouldn't tolerate any longer from clients, Kate plugged her energy leak and strengthened her energetic boundaries around time and money. She had better client relationships and her clients got better results.

Like Kate, when you stop your busy life (or realize it's not so scary) to deal with the legal parts of your business, you strengthen your boundaries in a powerful way that catapults you forward in your business. Without even thinking about it, you begin to attract clients and partners who operate at greater clarity and higher energetic frequency. It's a life-changing transformation.

The clearer your business boundaries are and the more they are spelled out in writing—like in your Client Agreement—the more you will attract people who are comfortable with boundaries—and the less you will feel yours are being violated. Putting boundaries in place equals raising your business vibe and attracting others who are operating at a similar energy frequency.

Fact: Using legal documents helps to identify, create and enforce your boundaries.

Identify Your Boundaries

If you don't know what your boundaries are, you don't know what to say in your legal documents. Identifying your boundaries is your first task.

It's critical that you know where you draw your lines in order to put them in writing. Often business owners don't even know what their boundaries are with their clients until they are tested. Trust me, it's better to figure them out now than wait until you're in a Legal Pickle.™

For example, if you offer one-on-one programs or services, you'll want to identify your boundaries in your Client Agreement around key areas like:

- Program description and benefits

- Expectations – both of you and your client

- Communication

45

- Scheduling appointments and cancellations

- Investment and Payment

- Refund policy

- Termination of your relationship

When you don't identify clear boundaries or think through the possibilities of what could go wrong, you sometimes discover your boundaries the hard way by giving refunds you don't want to give, returning texts on the weekends, or not being able to "fire" your client without losing thousands of dollars.

If you don't define your boundaries up front, for example, you may find yourself in sticky situations like these:

- You launch a 28-day jumpstart program, but you'd never thought about whether you wanted to give refunds—and now your client is asking for one. You've already spent the money, but you don't have a written Client Agreement so now you're feeling like you need to give the client the refund. Eeeeeks!

- You have a Client Agreement, but you didn't realize that when you said your program would include "unlimited e-mail and text support between calls" that a needy client would be texting you every day. You don't want to have to return e-mails or texts after 5 pm but your Client Agreement doesn't draw those lines. Your client keeps asking: "Why aren't you responding to my e-mails and texts???" Ugh.

- You used a generic agreement you found on the internet for your VIP Coaching Intensive but you realize now that it doesn't have any termination language to get out of the agreement if the client isn't a good match. Now you are stressed out because the client has been a nightmare with lots of demands on your time. You don't have any language that lets you out of the agreement because it's not personalized for your business. Whew.

These scenarios are not fun, yet coaches and entrepreneurs experience them daily because they don't have the right legal language in place and they haven't gotten clear about where they draw their boundaries.

Part of the role of a lawyer is to help you think through scenarios like these in advance and include language in your legal documents to help prevent them. That's why using a generic legal document designed for everyone prepared by a general attorney or online legal service isn't enough—you need to use legal documents designed specifically for your type of work by a lawyer who understands what you do. Otherwise, things fall through the cracks—like agreeing to respond to "unlimited emails and texts," including on nights, weekends and vacations.

Every entrepreneur or business owner draws different lines. Some business owners can't stand giving refunds. Some coaches love to give a "100% money back guarantee" if a client isn't happy with the program. Some entrepreneurs don't like voicemail, so they ask all client communication to be done by e-mail.

Boundaries can vary, and that's okay.

Typically, when you're just starting out, you may not be comfortable flexing your boundary muscles, so your boundaries tend to be more lenient. There's nothing wrong with that. The important thing is to get clear about where your boundaries are and know what feels good to you.

As your business expands, you may decide you don't want to give refunds and you switch over to a stronger refund policy. Or you may be like some coaches with million-dollar businesses who always offer 100% money back guarantees. It's totally up to you. Thinking through your boundaries up front is critical to protecting your time, energy, and money.

Create Written Boundaries

Once you identify where you draw your boundaries, you can put them in writing. I can't emphasize enough they need to be WRITTEN.

Boundaries that live in your head or that you jot down in your journal as you brainstorm for your new one-on-one program are not enough. You need to create words on the page in black and white to fall back on them, if needed.

When it comes to legal documents, I always say: "Less is not more. More is more."

Some business owners shy away from long legal documents. They feel more comfortable giving a shorter document to a client than a longer one, but when it comes to your protection, you don't want to short-change yourself. You don't want to use super-short documents with super-short terms because you think it will be better received. Your Client Agreement needs to be thorough and complete and it needs to not scrimp on language. Why? Because if you don't write the details in the document, it's much harder to enforce. If the language you need to fully protect isn't included in the document, you're out of luck.

Under the law, it's much easier to prove a boundary when it's in writing than when it is just spoken. It's not impossible, but it is far more difficult to piece together parts of e-mails and recollections of phone conversations than to use a single well-drafted agreement that contains all policies for your course or program. Bam. Right in one place.

Not only that, but most Client Agreements include a clause that says that what is written in the agreement is the "entire agreement" between you and the other person. This means that only what's written in the document is part of your agreement. This means that what's written on your sales page or added via e-mail is not part of your agreement unless it is WRITTEN in the agreement itself.

Give yourself the gift of protection: Use a legal document that contains thorough terms in one single written document.

Enforce Your Boundaries

The biggest benefit of all for using written legal documents is that they can help you enforce your boundaries. Once you've identified your boundaries and put them in writing, you now have written legal language to enforce if someone should challenge you or come after you. I like to say that you can let your legal document "do the heavy lifting for you."

Your written agreement is always what bears the greatest weight in a transaction. It's the first place that you as a business owner – and a judge or arbitrator - will turn to understand what you and your client agreed to in writing. In general, it's a primary form of evidence that can be used in court to show that your client agreed to your policies, so you want to be clear and thorough and have everything in writing.

Legally speaking, agreements are binding and enforceable when two things happen: (1) there is a meeting of the minds (this is when one person makes an "offer" and the other "accepts" it) and (2) a benefit of value is exchanged between the parties, such as services in exchange for money (which in legal-speak is called "consideration").

You want to use written agreements in your business so that you and your client are on the same page right from the start—and you have proof of your "meeting of the minds" and your exchange of money and services or products is crystal clear.

Having a signed agreement gives no wiggle room if your client comes back to you later to try to weasel out of it by saying, "But, I didn't see all of the terms of your agreement." Um, yes, the client did…because they signed the agreement. Even if they didn't read it or remember what it says, they are still legally bound by it because their signature is at the bottom of the page.

Are Electronic Signatures Allowed?

Yes, your clients can sign a Client Agreement with an electronic signature. In the United States, electronic signatures are permitted under the federal ESIGN Act provided that both parties agree in advance to use electronic versions of documents and sign electronically.

There are many electronic signature programs that you can use. (Some of my favorites are Adobe Sign, DocuSign, and HelloSign, but there are many great options.) Check for free trials, or you can sign up for monthly plans.

If signing electronically: Upload your agreement into the electronic signature platform, indicate where you want the other party to sign and date, and have it e-mailed to the other party who will electronically sign and date the document. Then it's your turn to e-sign it. Be sure to indicate that you want a signed copy e-mailed to both of you after you both have signed it.

> *Note*: Don't just e-mail your client a Word document or fillable .pdf that lets your client type in their name as their signature because anyone can access the document and type someone else's name. You need the electronic signature platform to serve as a reliable objective third party verifying your signatures.

If signing by pen: Send the agreement to your client as a .pdf document. Have them print out the agreement and sign the signature page with a ball point pen (blue is preferred) and then scan the entire document back to you, including the signature page. Then you sign it, make a copy and scan it back to the other party so the client also has a copy with both of your signatures.

> *Note*: You both should have a full document with the signed signature page so that no one can later argue that any changes were made after you both signed it. Be sure the ENTIRE document is scanned back to you—not just the signature page.

It's also wise to include language on the signature page that says "By signing below, you acknowledge, understand and agree to all of the terms of this Agreement." This gives you added protection that the client consented to everything that's written in the document.

When you get in a Legal Pickle®, you'll look to the terms of your agreement:

- If your client demands that you give a refund, you can rely on your written refund policy that says you give "no refunds" to back you up.

- If a client misses a call or a payment is late, you should look to your agreement to see whether a missed call is forfeited or may be made up within a particular time frame.

- If a client thinks that you promised "unlimited texts and e-mails" during your program and you don't remember making that promise, you'll turn to your Client Agreement to see what your program description includes.

See why having a written agreement is so important? It helps you avoid difficult and uncomfortable conversations with clients, and gives you the written backing to hold your ground and get out of those Legal Pickles™.

Your Legal Step: Your Client Agreement

When you are creating a new one-on-one program or service, there's no doubt, it can feel overwhelming and scary.

Maybe it's the first one-on-one program you've ever done. You're getting ready to roll it out and you're just not sure how to protect yourself. Or maybe you just did a beta test for a small group of hand-picked clients and now you are ready to launch it broadly. Or maybe it's your first high-end VIP Day and there's a lot of money at stake.

Use a Client Agreement for one-on-one programs and services.

(Note: Client Agreements are solely for one-on-one programs or services. If you're offering a group program, downloadable info product, physical product, or online course, you'll use Terms of Use which is covered in Chapter 5.)

Your Client Agreement is your go-to answer for protecting your "business baby"—your service that you have poured HOURS over to develop (not to mention the blood, sweat, tears and dollars) and the income that you plan to earn. Your hopes and dreams are all swaddled up in your program or services and you want to be sure you are nurturing and protecting them as much as you can.

Just like an expectant mother getting ready to bring new life into the world, you want to get clear about your expectations and philosophy about how you are going to begin and grow your client relationship right from the start.

Your written Client Agreement spells everything out in writing and gives you strong legal backing, which helps you feel safe, secure, and confident—and it creates clarity for both of you.

It's full of legal terms all tied up in a big red bow ready to hand to your clients to make both of your lives ten times easier when you start your work together.

When you …

- Spell out your policies IN WRITING, your clients feel safe and secure knowing your policies are clearly outlined for them.

- Gather your client policies IN ONE PLACE, your clients don't have to dig through their e-mails to remember your policies about refunds, missed appointments, or cancellations.

- Make your expectations CLEAR, your clients know how to show up for you (and themselves!) to get the results they seek. (Everyone wants a gold star!)

Most significantly, Client Agreements protect your income.

You have serious income to protect. Especially your biggest money-maker (like your VIP Day, Premium Package, or high-end program or service.) Your Client Agreement is where you spell out the services you are providing and the payment you'll receive.

Your Client Agreement is your friend. It's a friend both to you – and to your pocketbook. It's your ally, your sidekick, your partner in business.

Everything from whether you require a deposit, to whether payment may be made in lump sum or installments over time, where to send payment, when payment is due, whether you charge late fees, the types of payment you receive, and whether you allow for refunds is all laid out in your Client Agreement. It's your go-to legal language to cover your buns when it comes to money.

Using a Client Agreement is the best way to protect your income when working with private clients because it gives you language that you can enforce if payments are late or not made at all. A Client Agreement can help keep money flowing to you, and give you the written backing that you need.

A Client Agreement helps your CLIENTS know:

- What your expectations are for them

- What happens if they don't do their part (so there're no surprises later!)

- What they need to do to SHOW UP for you at their best

- What to do if they need to cancel or reschedule a call

- What happens if they miss a payment or want a refund

A Client Agreement helps YOU:

- Protect your income – this is the #1 reason to use a written Client Agreement

- Be clear about the services you are providing

- Prevent missed payments (so no more chasing down money!)

- Have a written refund policy that's super-clear

- Limit your liability because it contains your disclaimers and limitations

- Avoid headaches and awkwardness about missed calls or appointments

- Attract stronger clients by creating clearer Energetic Boundaries

Client Agreements are designed to help you and your client prepare for a healthy, happy experience together by creating clear communication right from the start about money, services, and every aspect of your work together.

Client Agreements are Gifts

I believe that Client Agreements are gifts to your clients.

When I mention this to entrepreneurs and coaches, it's often countered with, "Huh? Don't most people hate contracts?" You would think so, right? You would think that a written document full of "legalese" would not create "legal ease" at all.

But I beg to differ. Client Agreements are gifts to your clients—AND to you. Huge gifts.

If you're scared that you're going to e-mail a Client Agreement to a new prospect and they will take one look at it and back out—and then you will have no clients and no income and you'll be forced to close your business and never able to leave your dreaded day job, I totally get it.

I can see why you might be worried about that. After all, most legal documents are boring, confusing, and put you to sleep. Total snorers.

It can feel scary to use a Client Agreement—especially the first time you do it. But, trust me, you don't need to let those scary runaway thoughts overcome you.

Even if you're someone who thinks, "I love the idea of using a Client Agreement, but I'm terrified that my clients will freeze up or freak out if I hand them a harsh legal document."

What most lawyers don't tell you is that:

- Client Agreements don't have to be cold.

- Client Agreements don't have to be corporate.

- Client Agreements don't have to be scary.

I believe that a Client Agreement can be written with lots of Legal Love™; it doesn't have to be cold, corporate or scary. (I even use color in my Client Agreements. Totally shocking for a lawyer, I know.)

Client Agreements can be clear, kind documents that you share with your clients to help them feel safe and secure, without terrifying them when they see you coming. And, they can be super simple, easy to understand, and written in plain English.

Now, don't get me wrong—you still need to have some strong legal language in the document. After all, that's why you are creating it in the first place: to establish your boundaries. But the document can be written with warmth, in simple sentences, and still include the more legal-sounding sections that protect your rights, content, and intellectual property and limit your liability, disclaim certain things, and establish dispute resolution solutions.

Your Client Agreement can be both loving AND legally strong.

It can be an "AND."

How to Feel Good Using Client Agreements

If you're a bit squeamish about using a Client Agreement, here are 3 reasons why you can feel good about it:

1. **Client Agreements take care of your clients.**

Most business owners want their clients to feel comfortable right from the start. You want your client to know that they are going to be supported and stretched in a safe environment, and that you will take care of them throughout your entire relationship.

Your Client Agreement spells out the details of how exactly you will work together going forward. In fact, the client wants you to tell them what to do - really! When you tell the client right from the start what they need to do to be successful out of the gate, they feel relieved because they know what's expected of them.

The Client Agreement creates a container, or a structure, for caring for your client. Knowing the Agreement supports the concern you feel for your client lets you feel better using it.

2. Client Agreements help clients feel comfortable and safe.

Remember, the main purpose of the Client Agreement is to be clear about how you will work together. They're waiting for you to tell them what they need to do to be successful. They want you to give them instructions for how to interact with you. Believe it or not, direction provides comfort. Your Client Agreement gives your client that direction.

Clients easily can get overwhelmed with lots of details shared on the phone or in a discovery session, but having all of your policies in writing in one place to reference later gives them security and ups their trust in you.

When you lay out awkward details that can be uncomfortable to discuss—like handling late payments, missed calls, potential disputes—you help clients feel comfortable and safe by preventing ambiguity, confusion, or misunderstandings later.

Client Agreements create reassurance, comfort and safety.

3. Client Agreements feel good to use when you know what to say.

The way you present the Client Agreement will set the tone for the client's reaction. In other words, your client's comfort in receiving the Agreement is based on your confidence and tone when you present it.

For example, if you speak with ease and confidence, the client will accept the Agreement with ease. Conversely, if you are nervous or uncomfortable, the client will sense your hesitation and may feel uncomfortable as well.

Your job is simply to present the Agreement to the Client in a caring way. To do that, you just need to get into the right mindset. Focus on the fact you are giving the client two main gifts: (1) the gift of care, and (2) the gift of comfort, as discussed above.

When you're getting ready to send off a Client Agreement to a potential client, breathe deeply and feel in your heart that you are approaching your client from an open, warm, and loving place, just as you would when you approach them for a free discovery session or client session.

Your relaxed presentation of the Agreement will help the client to relax too. They watch your cues to determine how to react. They follow your lead. They pick up on your energy.

If you share the Client Agreement with peace and confidence, that's how it will be received by your client and that's what they will reflect back to you.

Okay, now that you're more relaxed and no longer freaked out about giving a Client Agreement to potential clients, you may be wondering, when should you use a Client Agreement?

When You Should Use a Client Agreement

Use a Client Agreement with programs and services for your one-on-one clients.

Anytime you are working with a private client in a one-on-one relationship, you need to use a written Client Agreement. Not only that, but you want to use a contract that is customized for each of your one-on-one programs.

Just so you know, the generic contract from your school or training program isn't going to cut it for long because it is designed for EVERYONE using your school's exact sample program. Unless you are using a generic cookie-cutter program with every single client, your contract won't cover the details of your unique programs.

You need to be sure it is tailored for each of your programs or services.

Can't I Use One Contract for Everything?

Nope! Using a single contract for all of your offers is not recommended. Using a different version of your Client Agreements for each of your one-on-one programs makes it easier to keep your offerings straight and avoids confusion and error.

How so? Because the terms are not the same for each program that you offer, the program description, the pricing, installment payments, cancellation, rescheduling, refund policy, and more can vary dramatically from program to program. If you're constantly revising the terms of your Client Agreement for each client or program, you could forget to include key language or accidentally delete parts that applied to one of your programs but not another—and then you'd be out of luck later if there's a dispute.

Many business owners don't realize that if they make a minor tweak to one section, it can affect multiple sections throughout the document. Having different version saved on your computer for each of your one-on-one offerings keeps things separate, simple, and safer for you. You'll just pull up the version that you need and send it off to your client to sign. You won't worry that you are making editing errors or missing parts that you need. Super-easy and done!

(Psss! If you make any edits to your Client Agreement, I highly recommend that you have an attorney review your changes so you aren't exposing yourself to risk without even knowing it.)

Don't Ever Guarantee Results

As a heart-centered entrepreneur or business owner, I know at times you can feel vested in your clients' outcomes. You want them to get the results they seek, give you raving testimonials and recommend you to all of their family and friends. That's understandable. However, you don't want to make any guarantees as to the results your clients will experience if they work with you.

Why? Because there is no possible way that you can ever guarantee their results, even if you wanted to.

Your job is to set them up with clear expectations about how they are to show up for themselves, how they are to interact with you and what their desired outcomes are... but you are not responsible for their outcomes. Let me be clear:

You are not responsible for your clients' results. Ever.

You're responsible only for providing the tools and support for helping them accomplish their own goals and your Client Agreement needs to reflect that.

As their coach, mentor, or guide, you are responsible for sharing tools and providing support, but you are NOT responsible for their weight loss or health improvements, their financial earnings increase or decrease, their sales, their website performance, or their anything!

How could you be responsible for your client when they're trying to lose weight and they go on a late-night snack binge? It's not like you're standing next to your client when they raid the fridge at midnight eating forkfuls of chocolate cake chased by swigs of milk, so how can you be responsible for their results?

You can't do the work for them.

It takes two to tango. Your role is to provide the container to guide and support them as they strive for success, but they need to show up for themselves to do the work. This means you can't take full credit for what they do accomplish, but the good news is that you can't be held responsible for where your client falls short.

Free yourself right now from this burden of carrying the responsibility for your clients. Set the burden down now. Take a deep breath and repeat after me: "My job is to provide the tools; it's their job to get the results." Don't you feel better already?

Remember, your only job is to empower your clients to be responsible for their own action, decisions and results, not carry their decisions for them—and you want to spell that out in Client Agreement.

Boundaries and Client Agreements
Align with the Sacral Chakra

Energetically, boundaries and Client Agreements relate to your second chakra, the sacral chakra, which is represented by the color orange.

The sacral chakra, or *Svadhisthana,* which means "dwelling place of the self," fills the space between the base of your spine and up to your belly button. It includes your pelvis, sacrum, and, if you're a woman, your womb.

I like to say that "all of the good stuff" is located in your sacral chakra. Principles affiliated with the sacral chakra include money, creativity, self-expression, joy, pleasure, relationships, sensuality, sexuality, and boundaries.

It's not by chance that we're talking about birthing programs in this chapter because birthing is connected to the sacral chakra. As an entrepreneur offering one-on-one programs, your creative offerings involve identifying, creating, and birthing your services into the world.

When you put a Client Agreement in place to protect your income, it helps you to plug your boundary leaks—like your money leaks, time leaks and energy leaks. Tightening up your Practical Boundaries and Energetic Boundaries allows your creativity and prosperity to flow in abundance and attract more money, clients, and abundance.

When we create boundaries, we can attract more of what we want.

When we align our decisions with our values and what's important to us, we focus our attention, time, and energy on our own needs, our own income, and our own joy. All that is not those things just falls away. We create more spaciousness, more freedom, and more room to receive more income. We attract more opportunities to do what fills our soul and more time with those we love. We fill up our fuel tanks so we have enough fuel to also care for others.

Not only that, but I believe that when we set clear boundaries and policies, we're better able to energetically attract those who will comply with our boundaries or policies. Those who value what we value will be drawn to work with us because we share a common belief system.

For example, those who want to work with socially responsible businesses will seek out and purchase goods from socially responsible businesses. Those who want to buy from heart-centered businesspeople will find themselves drawn to others whose "come from" is heart-centered too.

Simply put, like attracts like.

If you're needing a boost in supporting your sacral chakra, there are many things you can do to bolster this area of your body. One of my favorites is to recite this Sacral Chakra Mantra:

Sacral Chakra Mantra

When you are seeking more boundaries or abundance
in your life or business,
you can set your positive intention using this Sacral Chakra mantra:

"I am abundant. I am prosperous. I have firm boundaries."

Not only that, but when you set forth clear expectations and boundaries around how you work with your clients, you are strengthening your own energetic boundaries and drawing lines that allow you to stand as a leader in your business.

Your Client Agreement protects you in practical ways with written legal language to fall back on, and energetically, it supports your sacral chakra by raising your energetic frequency to attract more of what you want and expand your money, creativity, and abundance.

Now that we've talked about how to legally draw boundaries with your clients, let's address how to draw boundaries in your life and business… and why it's so darn difficult to do it.

Why is It So Freaking Hard to Set Firm Boundaries?

I realized that for healers, coaches, therapists, and heart-centered entrepreneurs, there seems to be one common theme. It's one of the biggest challenges for small business owners who like to love up clients and take pride in having flexibility and positive thinking. It's the Achilles Heel of being a coach or entrepreneur.

We have a tough time setting firm boundaries—or, truth be told, sometimes any boundaries at all.

We let clients miss calls. We let clients skip payments. Even if we do have a written agreement in place, we don't hold our clients to the contracts they signed. We reply to emails in the wee hours of the night, and we go way above and beyond what we stated in our program description. We let clients talk on and on and we don't end coaching calls on time because we don't want to hurt their feelings or cut them off in an emotional moment.

Sometimes, of course, it's totally appropriate to let a client finish a thought before concluding a coaching call, but sometimes we don't end a call because we don't have the backbone to wrap it up on time.

We don't want to appear cold or harsh or be too corporate or inflexible or anything else that we don't want to be.

We give and give and give.

Now, if you're sheepishly recognizing some of your own behavior as you read along, please be gentle with yourself. Cut yourself some slack for a moment. You are not alone. In fact, you are far from alone.

It can be challenging to say no. It's hard to draw lines. It's hard to enforce a boundary when someone is in need or depending on you. It's one of the hardest things to do in business—and in life. I have a hard time doing it at times, too.

When you have a big heart, it's hard to stop flowing conversations because you have another client call or your kids or spouse or parents or friends or pets need you. It's not always fun to interrupt and impose a boundary, and it doesn't always feel good.

Being Compassionate Is a Good Thing (Except When It's Not)

We generally think that having a big heart and being compassionate is a good thing to have in life—and in business. And it is.

Except when it's not.

When we overgive, overextend, and overstep in ways that negatively impact our income, our energy, our health or our family life, bad things happen.

Well, maybe not "bad," but things that aren't "ideal" or "desired" — things like not getting paid enough, not getting paid on time, or not getting paid at all.

We find ourselves apologizing to our next client for running late because we were still talking to our prior client and that doesn't make the start of the call feel very good for us or our client.

We end up giving away free information and advice because we're scared to ask for payment—especially from friends and family members. Why is it so hard to ask those people we love to pay for what we do? You'd think it would be easy because you know they are happy to support what you are doing, but sometimes it's even harder than asking clients.

Here's the bummer about overgiving: Flimsy boundaries end up costing us. Costing us a lot, like:

- Huge amounts of time.

- Thousands of dollars in income.

- Vast reserves of energy.

- Our sanity, integrity, and dignity.

- Even our livelihood.

Sometimes a boundary's gone before we even realized that being "nice and helpful" just cost us $2,500 in lost revenue because we didn't enroll that person as a client in our new program. Poof!

Or sometimes we have nothing in our bank account to show for the last 75 minutes of our discovery call (it was supposed to be 60 minutes, but we ran over by 15 minutes), other than the fact the person we helped gushed afterwards that they were "so, so grateful" for all of our help. We felt good about it—until we realized we should have charged them for the session.

Hmmm, why do we do this?

Why We Let People Take Advantage of Our Kindness

Why is it so hard to hold ourselves back?

Why does it seem so scary to ask for payment when we know that the value of the information we are offering is priceless and completely life-changing?

Why do we chose being nice over making a living?

Ohhhhh! That's right. It's because since we women were little girls, we're told that we should be nice and kind and helpful and quiet. No offense to the guys, but we women, especially, are told not make waves. We're told— both overtly and covertly—not to be disliked. Not to be excluded. Not to be talked about, not to be criticized, not to be a "bad girl," not to make people angry at us.

We're taught to be nice. We're taught to be pretty. We're taught to be quiet.

Moreover, we are taught that we're supposed to be nice *over* making money. We're taught that it's better to be viewed as "nice" than "greedy" or "money-hungry."

Wait—WHAT?

How did we learn that "nice" and "money" are positioned at opposite ends of the spectrum?

How come "being nice" and "making money" are viewed as polar opposites?

Are we really supposed to be nice over making money? Are we supposed to be nice rather than stand up for ourselves? Are we truly not supposed to make any waves? Really?

(As an aside, I am very curious to know if any man feels like he was taught as a child—overtly or covertly—to choose "nice" over "making money." I'm not citing any studies here but I am guessing that for the majority, the answer is likely "no.")

I always wonder ... why can't we be nice AND make money? Why can't we have people like us AND stand up for ourselves? Why can't we give amazing, loving coaching services in a 90-day program AND make $2,500? Or $25,000? Why can't we make our offers without feeling guilty for charging for our services or asking someone to pay for our knowledge?

Why can't it be an AND? Why does it feel like it needs to be an OR?

Honey, My Boundary's Sprung a Leak

I know from my own experience that when I overgive to others, my self-care becomes a huge boundary leak. I want to please my clients and not make them wait weeks for client appointment openings on my always-packed schedule, so I sacrifice time with my husband and my "me-time," and I forego some of the things that fill up my "love bank" the most—things like running, reading, and regular massages. I scratch them out and cross them off the calendar. It's not ideal. It's not smart. It's not how I want to live.

I am working on my boundaries too, just like everyone else. We all are works in progress.

What I know for sure is that when we don't have strong boundaries, they leak.

Flimsy boundaries easily can become cracked and permeable. The best of ourselves starts oozing through the cracks, and the next thing you know, we've given so much away that we have no time, energy, or love left for ourselves.

We sacrifice time with our families, time for our self-care, and time with our friends because we are exhausted and emotionally drained, and all we want to do is curl up on the couch and binge-watch *Orange is the New Black* while eating spoonfuls of mint-chocolate-chip-coconut-ice-cream. (Who does that? Who me? Oh no, not me!)

We find leaks with our money, our love, our energy, and our time because of this one simple fact: Those of us drawn to heart-centered entre-preneurship and coaching are pleasers.

We're givers. We're lovers. We're boundary-leakers.

Because we've been taught since we were toddlers just out of diapers to "play nice," "share," and "say you're sorry to your sister," we learn to take care of others' emotional states over our own. Somehow, over 20 or 30 years, this translates into us bending over backwards to make others feel good and loved up, and to put ourselves and our self-care last.

Until one day we wake up flat-out exhausted, unmotivated, and burnt out.

Or suffering from a health issue that forces us off our feet.

Or separating from our spouse because we've grown apart in recent years rather than continued to grow together.

It happens. There's no judgment in any of these events; they're just wake-up calls to change our behavior. Some wake-up calls come in whispers that we choose to ignore, and some come to us kicking and screaming. But they're all designed to get our attention to help us to stop the leaks, plug up the holes, and fill the gaps.

They come to tell us to stop catering to our clients, our work, our kids, our neighbors, our anything-that-needs-our-attention—and to please and love ourselves first.

Don't get me wrong— It's important to be loving and kind and polite and not try to hurt people's feelings, of course. Just like it's important for toddlers to learn how to share toys, play kindly with others, and apologize if they hurt someone. It's important to be kind.

But somewhere along the way, many of us big-hearted souls learn to reprogram our brain with putting others' needs first, rather than finding a way for our needs AND others' needs to co-exist. I am guilty of it too. I am all about loving my clients. Heck, my branding for my business is "Legal Love™," after all. I deeply value being loving and caring and supportive when it comes to my clients and the law, instead of being someone they think is going to be cold, intimidating, or scary...but sometimes that means I put clients before my own needs and I don't carve out time for my own self-care.

Somehow, we learn that taking care of us and taking care of others must be an "either/or" scenario—and not a "both/and" possibility.

This ends up looking like us having a hard time saying "no" to others ... and an even harder time saying "yes" to ourselves.

- We have a hard time saying to our friends, "Sorry, I can't make it" (without offering a million reasons for declining the invitation).

- We make up excuses for why we can't participate because it's just too darn scary to say, "This opportunity just doesn't align with my focus right now."

- We have a hard time saying no to clients because it feels next to impossible sometimes to say, even lovingly, "We need to wrap this call up because I have another client who's beeping in."

- We have a hard time telling a prospective client that, "You can take this farther with a new 90-day program I'm really excited about—and the investment is $1,497." Especially the first time we share this new offer with someone. (Scary!)

But here's the thing. If our fuel tank is on empty, we can't show up for ourselves or anyone else—and everyone loses.

That's why it's so important to get clear about our boundaries, set them, and stand behind them.

When we're clear about where we draw our lines, others will be clear too, and we will more often draw towards us, both physically and energetically, those who are aligned in thought and action.

This means that we will draw in and attract more dream clients, more aligned affiliates, more meaningful opportunities to showcase our work, and we will slow the attraction of those not paying us, not showing up on time, or not valuing what we do.

Sounds ideal, right?

The more we hone in on what we tolerate and don't tolerate, the more our external life and business will reflect that too. When we set clear boundaries, we free ourselves up for what's important.

From a material standpoint, we can set boundaries based on our beliefs, values, policies, and how we want to spend our time, energy and money, how we show up in your business and our lives.

While it can feel scary to set boundaries—especially at first—it doesn't have to be frightening. The more we do it, the easier it gets.

But sometimes you don't always know exactly what to say to be able to enforce your boundary. You just can't find the words and you don't want to be abrupt or hurt someone's feelings.

You feel like an awkward, pimply teenager with braces who isn't sure what to say when a boy asks her out. You don't know how to say you don't want to go to the dance with that boy because you have a crush on another boy who you really, really hope will ask you instead. You flub your words because you're trying so hard not to hurt him or embarrass him, but all you want to do is run away and pretend he never asked you in the first place.

Yes, it feels like that sometimes. Even when you're a grown-up adult. This is normal. You can be prepared for common scenarios by playing them out in your head and by having "Boundary Mini-Scripts" handy that you can turn to when establishing boundaries with your mate, your kids, and your clients and this can alleviate a lot of anxiety.

I'm going to be honest. The first time you tighten your boundaries and hold your ground with loved ones or clients, your palms may sweat. Your throat may tighten. You may stammer and "uh" and "um," and not fully get the words out without tripping over them. Your heartrate may race. It's all okay.

Stretching your boundary muscle is an act of courage and it takes practice.

Like a new yoga pose, at first you might not be so good at it. You may try to get into crow pose and wobble a bit. You may only get one leg perched on your bended arm, or you may topple forward onto your nose. It may take a few times before you find that sweet spot and balance in just the right spot to hold the pose with grace and ease.

Speaking and holding new boundaries is much the same. So break out your yoga mat, and let's get practicing. They call it a yoga *practice* for a reason. Only now you're heading into "boundary practice." Start with your deep pranayama breathing and get into the flow of setting new boundaries.

Key Takeaways from This Chapter

Just as the Client Agreement is the second legal step to take, boundaries are just one essential element for having a successful business as an entrepreneur. Identifying, creating, and enforcing your Boundaries is key for expanding your income, creativity, and abundance.

Your second legal step is to use a Client Agreement for your one-on-one services.

Your second soul-centered principle is boundaries.

Your second chakra that is supported and aligned is your sacral chakra.

Now It's Your Turn …

Use this Legal Checklist and Business Self-Assessment to jot down your thoughts to help you set your boundaries, get clear about your Client Agreement, and take legal steps so you can protect yourself, your business and your brand.

Legal Checklist:

1. Do you work with one-on-one clients?

2. Do you have a Client Agreement in place that is customized for each of your one-on-one programs or services? (If so, you get a gold star!)

3. If you don't have your Client Agreement yet, have you identified what's holding you back?

4. Do you have a clear refund policy?

5. Do you feel clients are taking advantage of your kindness and find yourself giving refunds, rescheduling appointments, or allowing late payments when you don't want to? (Don't worry, you're not alone!)

Business Self-Assessment:

1. Are you an overgiver? Do you find that you often overgive your time, expertise, and energy or not charge enough for your services?

2. Do you have boundary leaks? Money leaks? Time leaks? Energy leaks? Other leaks?

3. Do the boundaries you've set to date reflect your values, beliefs, and desires?

4. Have you found yourself in sticky situations where you've had a hard time enforcing your Boundaries with your clients, family, or friends?

5. Do you have your own "Boundary Mini-Scripts" of what to say to your spouse/significant other, kids and clients when you need to enforce a boundary?

Don't forget to grab your Legal Love™ Bonus Content!

Legal Love™ Bonus Content:

"5 Critical Components of Every Client Agreement"
Free download at lisafraley.com/clientagreementcriticalcomponents
($197 value)

Chapter 3.

Business Registration and Taxes.
Confidence. Solar Plexus Chakra.

If you're like a lot of my clients, you doubt yourself. All the time. Most of the time, when you're building your business, everything feels terrifying. Confident is the last thing that you feel when you are setting up your business and trying new things. Especially when starting out.

Confidence. We don't always feel that we have it, but we all desperately need it.

More often than not, if you're a high-achieving, motivated business owner, you probably second-guess everything you're doing—your e-newsletter, your logo, your branding, your website design, your free opt-in gift, your sales page design, your webinar formats, your home office setup, your course purchases, your course offerings...The list goes on and on.

You question and doubt whether what you are doing is "right" or "enough." It's easy to waste countless hours on Facebook or other businesses' websites seeing what they are doing and feeling crappy about yourself because you aren't doing exactly what they're doing—or even ANYTHING that they're doing. You beat yourself up. You don't feel very smart, or radiant, or confident ... like, ever.

I want to reassure you that you aren't the first to torture yourself with feeling "less than" or "not enough"—and you won't be the last. The "fraud factor" is real, for sure, and it's common to feel like you should give up and go back to your painful nine-to-five job rather than stay in this crazy online world.

Listen to what some of my clients have told me:

- "I've put so much work into this new website but I am scared to press 'publish' because everyone will see it. What if they don't like it or no one goes to it? I'll feel like I've totally failed."

- "I've created a new four-week program but I am not sure if I am giving enough value to people. I'm scared to price it too high because then no one will buy it, so I have added five bonuses to what they are already getting in the program. Do you think $197 is too much to charge?"

- "I'm hanging out my shingle as a business coach and have my first discovery call to enroll a client, but don't I need to register my business or do something official first? I'm afraid that I'll get in trouble with the government or the IRS will come after me."

- "I had professional photos taken for the first time. It was such an upleveled experience to work with a stylist, get my hair and makeup done, take photos in a real studio, and have a professional photographer make me look and feel beautiful—but I am scared to show people the photos because it feels so vulnerable. I feel really exposed." (Oh wait, that wasn't a client - it was me!)

Sound familiar? Insecurity shows up all over the place. Let me reassure you: It's totally expected and natural to feel that way.

Becoming an entrepreneur and leaving the safety and security of a steady paycheck that comes with a nine-to-five day job—even a job you hate—is one of the scariest things most entrepreneurs have ever done. I know it was for me. It's a huge stretch to leave your day job and that secure income—everything you've ever known in the work world—and create something on your own at your kitchen table, extra bedroom, or in a coffeehouse while drinking lattes.

For me, building a business from the ground up using a laptop, a cell phone, and a prayer is one of the most challenging ventures I have ever undertaken—which says a lot considering I have done other things most people would consider "hard"—like pass the bar exam, travel to Europe by myself, run three marathons (including one in 25° weather!), get a job in the White House, and dress up for a fancy dinner at Le Cirque in Las Vegas and order a table for one.

Sleep-Depriving Fears and Worries

There are so many worries and fears that keep entrepreneurs up at night like:

- What if I don't make any money?

- What if I do my first big launch and only two people sign up?

- What if a client thinks that I don't really know what I'm talking about?

- What if I don't know the answers to my client's questions?

- What if I don't do it right?

- What if my parents/spouse/friends are right that I shouldn't have quit my day job?

- What if I get too big that I don't have time for my kids?

- What if I become successful and then it somehow all goes away?

- What if I set up my business wrong and I have to shut it down and go back to work?

The worries and doubts that creep into our minds when we're trying to get some shut eye freak us out and keep us playing small.

I'm not going to sugar-coat it. It's scary to take the leap into entrepreneurship and to trust that the net will catch you.

Building a business requires that you dig deep and draw on your inner confidence, power, and strength to help you move forward, one day at a time, taking baby step after baby step to build the business of your dreams.

What Does It Mean to be a Sole Proprietor?

When you're a solo business owner – a one-person show - you're called a Sole Proprietor. You don't have to do anything special to earn that title; you just start a business and get paid for your goods or services.

Being a Sole Proprietor is the simplest and least expensive way to get started.

Unless you have a lot of personal assets, starting out as a Sole Proprietor is easy. You give your business a name and start operating the business and instantly you're considered a Sole Proprietor. That's the good news.

However, as a Sole Proprietor, all business responsibilities and decisions are made by you, which means that you're completely responsible for the all income, expenses, assets, debts, legal responsibilities and liability of the business as a solopreneur.

The drawback as a Sole Proprietor is that you do not have a formal business entity to protect you. It's just you. Hence, your personal assets are not shielded from the claims of business creditors, and you have limited tax planning options because you and your business are legally one and the same.

This means your personal assets are not separated in any way from your business assets, so if someone comes after you and sues you in your personal life, they are not prevented from accessing your business assets like your business bank accounts or equipment. The same is true vice-versa. If someone sues you for a business situation, they can also potentially access your personal assets like your house or your car. This leaves you legally exposed. That's the bad news.

The Pros and Cons of Sole Proprietorship

The benefits of Sole Proprietorship are:

- Super simple to create—just file a few documents

- Little maintenance required

- Quick to establish

- Inexpensive

- The downsides of Sole Proprietorship are:

- No limitation of liability (so your buns are exposed)

- No tax savings—must pay self-employment tax (basically Social Security and Medicare taxes)

- No legal protection

Note: This is not an exhaustive list. It just highlights some of the key pros and cons.

Because you haven't formed a business entity like a limited liability company (LLC) or S-corporation yet, the income that you make from your business is combined with any other source of personal income (like a day job or other part-time jobs) and it all is susceptible to creditors.

When it comes to filing your taxes, as a Sole Proprietor, you'll list your business income and expenses on your individual tax return. Because you work for yourself, you'll also be responsible for paying self-employment taxes. (I highly recommend that you have an accountant calculate and prepare your tax returns, no matter how large or small of a business you own. Personalized attention, accurate calculations, and peace of mind are worth every penny no matter how simple or complex your business may be.)

Getting started as a Sole Proprietor is super-easy, but you still need to pay your taxes and take steps to let the government know that your business exists and that you are making money. When you put legal steps in place for your business and you register your business properly, you're laying the groundwork for success.

Let's dive a little deeper into business registration and taxes, and then we'll explore feeling confident as a business owner, especially on those days when you want to throw in the towel.

Your Legal Step: Business Registration & Taxes

Many clients have come to me because they have no idea how to properly set up their business. Some do it on their own and then worry that they didn't file the right documents and they'll get shut down. They worry and fear that they:

- Don't have the correct—or any!—legal documents in place to protect themselves

- Don't know if they've set their business up properly

- Don't know if they're not saving enough to pay for taxes

- Don't feel confident that the government, IRS or an irate client won't come after them

- Don't know if they should form an LLC or S-Corp or whether they should remain a Sole Proprietor

When you don't know what to do or you aren't sure whether you've set your business up correctly, you feel legally naked and exposed, which isn't a fun feeling.

When you start your business as Sole Proprietor, there isn't a business manual with super-simple instructions that drops from the sky so you know how to set yourself up properly. (Wouldn't it be nice if it did?) You likely have no idea if you are supposed to file paperwork, pay fees, or let the government know you have income so you can pay taxes and act like a "real" business. You probably weren't taught about these legal and financial responsibilities in your business school or training program.

Part of the "fraud factor"—feeling like a fraud in your business—happens when you don't show up as a powerful and responsible leader of your business. It's easy to feel like an imposter in the business world if you haven't set yourself up correctly as an operating business ... whether you're running your business from rented office space or your dining room table.

When you register your business and get clear about taxes, you feel self-assured and legitimate as a "real" business owner.

You shift from having a very expensive "hobby" to being a full-fledged business owner.

My clients tell me how much better they feel when they file their local, county, and/or state business registration documents and file their first business tax return. Not to mention they no longer worry that the government will come and track them down. They may not like paying taxes, but they like being in integrity with the law.

When Should You Register Your Business and Deal with Taxes?

The short answer: File your documents and get clear about taxes once you are making income.

If you have even one paying client as a Sole Proprietor, you now have income. Congratulations! It's thrilling the first time you are paid for your services or products in your very own business. It's also time to let the government know you're officially making money.

No matter where your business is based, each city, county, state, and country has different requirements to follow, but they all require you to declare that you're in business and report your income. Whether you're a Sole Proprietor or you have a business entity like a limited liability company (LLC) or S-Corporation, you need to register your business and pay your taxes. (Corporate entities like LLCs and S-Corps are covered in Chapter 6.)

Start your business on the right foot by registering your business properly and paying your taxes – even when you are just starting out.

Do I Have to Report My Income If I Only Have 3 Clients?

Every so often, I get asked if income needs to be reported when you have only a few paying clients. Some biz owners think they are too small for their tiny income to matter much to the government in the early days of business-building.

Here's the deal though: Just as I tell every client, if you've received any business income at all – even from 3 clients - you need to report it. Otherwise, it's considered tax evasion.

Yep! Tax evasion. (That sounds scary, right?)

It is scary. I'm not trying to startle you or shame you if you haven't been up front about the initial income you've received from clients, but I do want to emphasize the importance of being in integrity with the law – not to mention your values – as a business owner.

No matter how much or how little you've received from clients as payment for your services, you need to report it on your tax return.

Yes, even if it was only a "practice" client and they paid you $25.

Yes, even if it's only $150.

Yes, even if you've only had 3 clients.

It's important that you step up and do your part in paying your business taxes. It truly doesn't matter how much money you've made.

Since I'm guessing that you'd describe yourself as a woman (or man) of integrity with strong values as a heart-centered entrepreneur or business owner, I suspect that you want to do what's right and comply with the law. Not only is paying taxes legally required, but it's in alignment with your values and it's the right thing to do. As my mother would say, "it's the principle of the matter."

And, of course, it's the law.

When it comes to business registration and taxes, you may be wondering:

- What documents do I need to file with my city, state, or country?

- Do I need a business license?

- Do I need to pay any fees?

- Do I need to file a "DBA" (doing business as)?

- What do I need to know about taxes?

- Should I hire an accountant?

What you need to do for business registration and taxes is based on where you live, where your business is based, and the specific kind of business you have. Not only that, but the law on the local, state and federal levels can change at any time, so the forms and the fees also may shift at any time.

Everyone's business is unique and what documents you need to file vary by location. What's required for you may not be required for someone else in your field who's in a different city.

What that means for you is if you're a business owner in San Francisco, for example, you likely need to file different documents than your friend who owns a business in New York City. Not only that, but the forms you file this year may be slightly different than those you filed last year.

This makes it hard to list the forms you need based on where you're located, but I can tell you about common business registration forms and registration fees that may apply to you.

In the United States, almost every city and county requires that you register your business and pay a registration fee, and likely at least a small tax. In general, taxes are lower at the local level and higher at the federal level.

There's a strong chance that you'll need to file forms at the federal, state, county and/or local government levels- no matter what kind of business you own.

Please note that this list of forms is not exhaustive, nor does it mean that each of these forms apply specifically to you. These are examples of what forms might be required at the state, county and local levels. (If you are located outside of the United States, you'll want to inquire at your local, county, state/province and national levels too.)

At the national level, you'll pay federal taxes and complete numerous forms. Most Sole Proprietors will need to complete many of these forms – and maybe also others not listed:

Federal Government / Internal Revenue Service

1. Income Tax Forms (and possibly Estimated Tax Forms)

2. Sole Proprietor Tax Forms

3. Social Security, Medicare & Income Tax Withholding Forms

4. Federal Unemployment Tax (FUTA)

5. Excise Taxes

6. Employer Identification Number (EIN) / Federal Tax ID Number (optional, unless have employees)

At the state level, Sole Proprietors also need to pay state taxes, and you may need to file additional forms if your business name is different than your legal name or if you sell goods or products that are subject to sales tax:

State Government

1. "Doing Business As" / Fictitious Name / Trade Name Form

2. Business Registration Form

3. Sales Tax Forms

4. Franchise or State Tax ID Forms (required in some states)

5. Business License (depending on the type of business)

When Should I File a "Doing Business As" (DBA) Form?

I'm often asked when you should file a "doing business as" form and where you need to file it.

A DBA (which also may be called a Fictitious Name or Trade Name in your state) Form is used when the name of your business differs from your personal legal name.

The purpose of the DBA Form is to let the government know that you and your business are related. If the name of your business is not the same as your personal name, you are required to inform the government of the connection.

Let's look at a few examples:

1. Rachel Rockstar is a Sole Proprietor who calls her business "Better Body Now." Rachel likely will need to file a DBA at the state level, (and check if needed at the county and local levels too.) Why? Rachel needs to tell the state that her business is called "Better Body Now" to register her business and pay taxes.

2. Douglas Dogood owns "Doug's Donuts". Doug would need to file a DBA because the state would not be able to tell that Doug Dogood and "Doug's Donuts" are connected unless Doug files the proper paperwork.

3. Lucy Luckystar is a life coach with a business called "Lucy Luckystar Coaching." Because Lucy's full legal name is in the title of her business, Lucy may NOT need to file a DBA at the state, county or local levels, but she needs to find out since "Coaching" is also part of her business name.

Each city, county and state is different and the requirements vary so find out what you need to do for your business specifically.

Some counties also require that DBA and business registration forms be filed, and perhaps other forms too:

County Government

1. "Doing Business As" / Fictitious Name / Trade Name Form

2. Business Registration Form

Most local governments require forms to be submitted too:

Local Government (City / Town / Village)

1. "Doing Business As" / Fictitious Name / Trade Name Form

2. Business Personal Property Tax Form

3. Business License (depending on the type of business)

4. Franchise Tax Form

5. Zoning and Land Use Forms

6. Waste Disposal Forms

7. Home-Based Business Forms

8. Other Forms (specific to the type of work that you do)

Whew! That's a long list! Don't let the number of forms freak you out. You likely only have to file a fraction of them, but you need to file the right ones.

It's your responsibility as a business owner to find out what forms are required for your business and to file them, submit your registration fees, and pay taxes. The best way to do that is to call your local, county and state government offices or research them online to determine what documents and fees are required for a Sole Proprietor in your area.

Determine Where Your "Business Office" is Located

What documents you need to file will depend on where your business office is located. How do you determine where your business office is located?

As a Sole Proprietor, your business office is generally located at the address where the bulk of your work is conducted.

If you work primarily from home, your home address would most likely be your business office address (even if you frequent the local coffeehouse with your laptop and earbuds daily.) If you rent office space, your office building likely would be used for your business office address.

Regardless whether your clients are located across the globe, your business office is located at the address where your business is headquartered – which is most likely where you keep your computer, desk and business files. Many online entrepreneurs serve clients from all over the world, but their home office (or kitchen table) is where the business is based.

What if you're a self-described "nomad" who lives in Colorado for 3 months, Bali for 3 months, Hawaii for 3 months and Paris for 3 months? Which location qualifies as your business office? Talk with an accountant to make that determination and file your business registration documents accordingly.

For business registration, it's wise to have a lawyer assist you, and for taxes, you'll want an accountant on your team.

I highly recommend working with a local attorney to file your business registration and be sure you are paying the proper fees. You want to be sure you are filing the right documents and in the right format (online or hard copy), paying the correct registration fees, and you're aware of any annual reports or renewal fees that you'll need to pay on an ongoing basis. Some cities, counties, and states require a lot of paperwork; others require very little.

It's well worth the time and expense to have a lawyer get your "official" documents registered and a trusted accountant who can help you with business planning and taxes.

(If you're unsure what to ask when you're hiring an accountant, grab the "Top 10 Questions to Ask When You're Hiring an Accountant" Checklist in the Legal Love™ Bonus Content at the end of this chapter.)

As I've mentioned, as a Sole Proprietor, you and your business are treated as one and the same for tax purposes. What that means is that your personal income is combined with your business income and is reported and taxed collectively. An accountant can help you make sure you are reporting your income correctly and using the proper forms and help avoid an IRS audit or inquiries.

You feel more confident when you know you are following the law and operating your business legally. You feel proud and relieved knowing that you are acting like a responsible business owner, hiring experts to do the heavy lifting, and you stand in your integrity.

Even if you are working from your guest bedroom.

Even if you are only working part-time or just starting out.

Even if you think you are "too small" to need it.

Not only that, but when you take your business more seriously, you find that clients and other business owners take you more seriously.

Surprised? I'm not.

Have you ever noticed that when you start showing up more powerfully and professionally in your work, others show up more for you?

It's amazing how that works.

When you file legal documents and show up in alignment with your values, you begin to attract more ideal clients and more opportunities to showcase your work. Your increased professionalism raises your business frequency because you are operating in integrity with yourself and the law.

You stop feeling paralyzed by fear and you start taking action because you feel confident and capable. When you get legally covered on the business front, you show up, play bigger, and attract opportunities that lead you into the next level of your business—which is exactly what you want.

Confidence and Business Registration & Taxes
Align with the Solar Plexus Chakra

Energetically, the third chakra—the solar plexus chakra— is aligned with being empowered and confident as a business owner and taking responsibility by filing your business documents properly and paying taxes. The solar plexus is located at your core in the center of your body.

The third chakra is located between the navel and the solar plexus in the abdominal region. In Sanskrit, the solar plexus is called *Manipura*, which means "city of jewels" or "lustrous gem," as if to describe something so precious and valuable. That tells you how important it is.

The solar plexus is the center of our willpower, self-esteem, and self-confidence, and it's the anchor for our identity, power, confidence and ego. It's the seat of our sense of self. This is the chakra where we harness and use our internal strength and personal power to move forward and take action in our life and business.

It's not by chance that our inner core is aligned with our third chakra. The core gives ballast and energetic stability. When you have a strong core and your energy is centered in your body, you may notice you feel more balanced and centered. When you stand tall and hold your head high, you don't lean too far forward to overgive (which is excessive masculine energy) or lean back too far to over-receive (which is excessive feminine energy.)

We're going to explore the many ways to find your confidence when it seems to be waning throughout the rest of this chapter, but in the meantime, if you need a little confidence pick-me-up, this Solar Plexus Mantra can help:

Solar Plexus Chakra Mantra

When you are seeking more confidence in your life or business, you can set your intention with this Solar Plexus Chakra mantra:

"I am confident. I am powerful. I am capable. I am aligned."

The third chakra also houses what we commonly call our "gut instinct"—our intuition. When we have that funny feeling in our gut that something feels "off" or that we don't think it's safe to get into a car with a friend who's had one too many cosmopolitans, that's our gut instinct talking.

Your gut instinct—or gut reaction—probably has saved you many times in your life from a bad decision or catastrophic accident. Everything from not making an impulse purchase of yet another online program that you don't truly need to saying no to dating a guy who you met on Tinder can be as result of listening to your intuition or experiencing a gut reaction.

Often when we follow our gut instinct, we have no tangible physical evidence that tells us to be worried or fearful, but our intuition has us on guard "just because" something doesn't feel right.

Our gut always has our back—though we don't always listen to it or honor what it nudges us to do—like when we go out with that guy anyway and later find ourselves sobbing over a glass of wine (or kombucha) because he ended up being such a jerk.

The Gut is the Seat of Vulnerability

When I was a little girl, I used to watch boxing on TV on Saturday afternoons with my dad. I remember watching those boxers repeatedly hit each other in the gut and I'd wonder how they had the energy and strength to get up and fight after being knocked down again and again.

It's not by chance that when boxers start throwing punches that they so often give an uppercut sucker-punch right into the abdomen which can drop their opponent to the floor. *Wham.* They're down for the count. A physical punch in the gut can cripple even the most accomplished boxer and take them out of the fight. That's why core strength is so important.

I believe that confidence is closely tied to having a solid core.

Having core strength is strongly tied to a healthy gut, which is important physically, emotionally, and energetically.

As a health coach, I learned through my training that our gut influences our physical health and emotional health in a few other ways. The core of our body is the center of our immune system. According to a study published in the *American Journal of Physiology* shared by the National Center for Biotechnology Information, U.S. National Library of Medicine, "the gut immune system has 70-80% of the body's immune cells".[4] These immune cells line our digestive system and are critical for fighting and preventing illness and disease.[5] Healthy gut flora are critical for breaking down food, processing and absorbing nutrients for our cells to use, eliminating waste, and keeping us healthy. We literally can't survive without a healthy gut.

We can't survive emotionally either.

The gut is where the majority of our neurotransmitters are used that affect our mood and temperament. Neurotransmitters are substances that transmit nerve impulses across a synapse between neurons. The gut has been nicknamed the "second brain" by scientists. While the gut doesn't process cognitive or conscious thoughts like our brain does, as part of the enteric nervous system, it does contain 100 million neurons that impact our mood.[6]

If our "second brain" is not in balance, our mood and emotional health can be affected. I certainly can attest to that.

I have a confession to make when it comes to the gut.

I Used to Be a Sugar Addict

It took me years before I got up the courage to publicly acknowledge that I was a sugar addict. I used to feel so much shame about the fact that for years I was addicted to sugar. Sugar used to be the fuel—and the emotional crutch—that got me through long work days. I would eat the big bags of peanut M&Ms, sleeves of crackers, and boxes of marshmallow bunnies. (Oh, how I loved those yellow marshmallow bunnies!) I ate sugar every single day until I was age 40. In reality, it was multiple times a day. Sugar was my friend and constant companion and helped me get through workplace stress, boyfriend breakups, and daily life.

While I didn't have a big weight problem, I could NOT stop eating sugar.

To make matters worse, as a Type-A overachiever, I was hard on myself. I would beat myself up about how much sugar I ate, and how often I ate it. I would get frustrated that I could do challenging things like land a high-powered job in a big law firm, but I could not make myself stop eating sugar.

At the time, I had no idea that sugar was even addictive—and that I am sugar-sensitive.

At one point, I remember being utterly horrified and panicked at the mere thought of going a day without sugar. But one day when I was hiking in the glorious Canadian Rocky Mountains with my husband and parents, I decided that I was going to stop eating sugar. For six months. For real. At least, I was going to try.

Before I went cold turkey, I gave myself permission for a "last hurrah" to eat as much sugar as I wanted during that trip, and not judge myself for one bite of it.

You wouldn't believe how much sugar I ate. Foods that I hadn't touched in decades, like pink-frosted donuts from a local bakery, ridiculously decadent desserts at the Fairmont Chateau Lake Louise, handfuls of candy bars, and boxes of maple sugar candy—all without restricting or judging myself at all.

Not surprisingly, I gained a few pounds and my mood was bonkers from the crazy sugar highs and lows, but I realized it was the first time in my life I was free from self-judgment for what I put into my mouth. I hadn't even realized how much I used to judge myself until I allowed myself to eat without any judgment. It felt like total freedom.

Not judging myself during that vacation was one of the most liberating things I have ever done.

I came home from the trip and I committed to using only stevia and fruit as my sources of sweetness for the next six months. That means I had no birthday cake, no mint chocolate chip ice cream, and no peanut M&Ms. None of my favorite sweet treats. Nothing. For six months.

I never thought I could do it.

But I did it. I gave up sugar entirely for six long months.

I went from feeling controlled by sugar to realizing that sugar was something that I was free to choose. I got my freedom back—and at the same time, I regained my sense of power which dramatically impacted my confidence.

Instead of feeling like I was at the mercy of sugar cravings that needed to be satisfied at least five times a day, I added sweetness into my life other ways. I ate more fruit. I exercised more—but, for once, not to punish myself for eating too much sugar.

I spent more time with friends and filled my life with love and sweetness in other ways. I started holding hugs for 20 seconds with my husband (yes, at first, we timed them!) to incite the natural production of more oxytocin, nature's happy drug.

I boosted my self-care with regular massages and manicures. I opened to more love from my husband, my family, my friends, my colleagues, my cats, and random strangers I talked to in the grocery store.

I realized that what I ate impacted my mood tremendously and my entire demeanor changed when I started to honor myself, my body, and my gut feelings more often.

I lost weight, I felt more in control and I felt more confident. All from giving up sugar.

Until I went through my sugar-busting experience, I had no idea that sugar was so profoundly affecting my mood and how I felt about myself. I had no idea that the sugar was sabotaging my confidence – and probably had been negatively impacting it for years - and that I could consciously choose to do something about it.

I had no idea that I could change my gut and my core, and resultingly, I could change my life.

Now, I feel free to choose sugar whenever I want and not feel controlled by it. Sugar doesn't own me anymore. I don't say "no" every time—and I don't say "yes" every time either. It's not an "either/or" anymore—now it's an "and." I do have to eat it consciously so I don't cross the line into triggering old cravings, but I enjoy it in small doses.

I strongly believe that the gut is at the core of our health. The health of our physical bodies, our emotional well-being—and, yes, also our businesses.

Your Body, Your Energy & Your Business
(Psst! They're All Related)

Though it may not seem to be the case at first glance, your body, your energy and your business are all just reflections of the same thing—your inner core. They all affect how you:

- Carry yourself in the outside world

- Perceive yourself

- Are perceived by others

- Define your sense of self and who you are

- Hold your sense of self-esteem, pride, confidence, power, will, and responsibility.

How you carry your body, express your energy and show up in your work reflects what you believe about yourself deep inside your core - and it gets mirrored on the outside in your life and business.

For example, one day during a recent Spiritual Mastermind session, one of my friends, Christine Callahan-Oke, saw me in our Zoom video classroom and said, "Lisa, you're beaming right now. You look absolutely radiant. There are beams of light shining out of you and you are lighting up the room with your presence."

Huh? Wha ...? What was she talking about?

That's quite a compliment. I had no idea I was beaming or radiant or lighting up the room with my presence. In fact, I was sitting in my home office in my comfy clothes in front of my laptop with bad lighting on a cloudy day. I didn't feel I was "beaming" in any way.

I do remember I was feeling good that day. I had just finished a launch for my online legal course called "get legally covered so you can go bare." I was happy with the results and excited for the course to start. I was in a positive mental spot.

When I questioned Christine about why she thought I was "beaming" (when I was dressed more for watching movies curled upon the couch than for going out into the world), she said that she could tell that I was feeling happy and proud and confident. Since I was filled up on the inside, she couldn't help but to notice that my positive energy overflowed to the outside.

Interesting.

One way to know that you have a strong core on the inside is that your confidence, strength, and self-esteem show on the outside.

That got me thinking, though. There are days when we know we feel confident. We walk around with our shoulders back, chin up and standing tall. And then there are days when we feel crappy. We think we're failing at our business. We worry no one will buy our programs or services. We fear we'll have to return to our dreaded day job. We don't feel confident at all. We have no mojo.

But what about all the days when we're in between and we can't recognize the radiance that other people see in us? What then? How can we tell if we're more "solid" on the inside than we think we are—especially when we're mired in doubt and confusion in our business?

I'm talking about situations like where Christine told me I was radiant and I had no idea what she was talking about. If someone else can see us "beaming" with radiance, we probably have more confidence than we think we do, right?

What if My Core Has a Muffin Top?

If you're like me, you have been tough on yourself – and your core! - at one time or another for having a "muffin top" or a "stomach pooch" or a "beer belly."

You may have looked in a full body mirror and told your friends or spouse (or even your cat) "how fat I look in these jeans." You may have criticized the way you looked when trying on bathing suits and felt self-conscious about your body.

In fact, if you're a woman, I almost guarantee that you have beaten yourself up about your body in one way or another at some time in your life. (If you're a man, you may have too.)

We women are relentless though, particularly to our core - and about our core.

We are constantly bombarded with suggestions how to lose ten pounds by Friday, look hot and sexy tonight, and get better abs without doing any sit-ups.

Some women use exercise programs, diet plans, and weight loss pills to help lose belly fat. Some go under the knife to get liposuction or a tummy tuck. Some go to the lingerie department to hold their belly in with super-tight-fitting Spanx.

When we may see the extra 15 (or 50) pounds we want to lose when we look in the mirror, we know that our inner confidence is tucked into the waistband of our jeans too.

We all need to be gentle with ourselves. Even if we're lamenting the extra belly bulge that's disguising our confidence and strong core, we need to remember that both are still there. They may just have to be uncovered a bit, but underneath it all, they're still there.

Now that you have a general sense how to recognize core strength and confidence, let's talk about how you feel confident in your life or business on those days (or months) when you don't feel so hot.

How to Feel Confident When You Don't Feel So Confident

This topic is a biggie. As I was writing this book, I realized it was important not only to address core strength, but to share tools for how to feel confident and radiant when you're feeling stuck or small or shy.

Even if you don't think you're feeling very empowered or secure, let me assure you that you already have a vast reserve of confidence you can rely on to help you—even if you think it's vanished or you can't seem to find it.

Just like my Mastermind sister Christine who told me I was "beaming" and "radiant" that day when I didn't see myself in that light, other people can see your inner light and remind you who you are deep inside your core. Thank goodness for that!

The next time you're feeling scared or worried or doubting your incredible talent and abilities, don't worry. I've found six simple techniques that can help your confidence return again and again, just like a sunrise.

As you read each technique, keep an open mind. Try one or more of the techniques, choose those that resonate most for you, and leave the rest behind. Experiment. Set an intention that you want to uncover the confidence that's already deep within you, and take a few action steps to move your business forward.

6 Simple Techniques to Feel Confident Now

1. Stop Beating Yourself Up.

Stop whatever you're doing and take a deep breath. Put your hand on your heart and breathe in, then breathe out. Take three deep breaths.

Next, make a little pact with yourself that as of this moment, you'll stop beating yourself up. You'll stop talking yourself out of things. You'll stop telling yourself that you aren't good enough or smart enough or important enough or anything enough. You'll be open to getting out of your head and bringing yourself back into this present moment through your breath. You'll put your inner critic on pause and stop the internal ranting that's driving you nuts.

Believe me when I tell you this: NO ONE feels like they are enough. Not one person on this planet is enough or has enough of everything. No one.

Trust me when I say that exactly where you are right now, you are enough.

In this moment, you're right where you are supposed to be and you have so much to offer the world right now. Exactly as you are. However much you know or don't know, however many certifications you have or don't have, please stop beating yourself up. Where you are now makes you perfectly poised for your next step.

I will guarantee that you already know enough to take a tiny baby step to move forward in your business and to help others improve their lives – or it's easy for you to find out.

2. Remember Who You Are.

On those days when I feel down or I'm don't feel like I am enough (because, believe me, I am hard on myself too!), my dear friend and creative marketing director, Heather Jernigan, always says to me: "Let me remind you of who you are." I love that concept, and every time she does it, I remember and my confidence returns.

When we're shoulder-deep in our own fears, tears, and worries, it's easy to be short-sighted. We aren't able to see our own strengths and abilities.

During those times when Heather and I get on the phone, she reminds me of my positive attributes and accomplishments that reflect the core of who I am. For example, she'll say something like:

"Lisa, one of the things I admire about you is that you come from such a heartfelt place when you work with your clients. Unlike most lawyers, you love up your clients from an emotional place and support them with the care of a coach while giving them the tools of a lawyer. You make the law easy, approachable, light and fun—and your clients can feel how much you really care about them—which they never expect from a lawyer—and that's why they adore you and keep coming back to you for more."

See? How can you not feel good when someone tells you such nice things about yourself?

Whenever I'm bummed out that "my list is too small" or "my income isn't a million dollars" or whatever might be bothering me, Heather's kind words remind me of who I am at my core. She reminds me of what I value and how I approach my work, which shifts my thinking and energy from a scarcity mindset to one of abundance and gratitude, and my whole demeanor shifts.

Using this technique of remembering who you are can instantly uplevel your mindset to bring your attention back to the core of who you are so you feel more confident again.

3. Celebrate Your Wins.

Take a moment to celebrate your recent big wins and your teeny-tiny steps forward in your business and allow yourself to fully honor what you've accomplished. Acknowledge what you've checked off your to-do list to expand and grow your business.

When you are in a space of doubt and insecurity and you take a moment to celebrate what you have done that felt scary in the past, you can feel proud of yourself. Own your wins (big and small) and remind yourself of what you've already accomplished.

In this fast-paced, 24-hour news cycle and one-second-attention-span universe, we rarely take the time to let ourselves bask in the glory of our work after we accomplish a goal. We're so quick to dismiss our win, check it off the list, and move on to the next task that we forget to appreciate how much we've achieved.

Celebrate the fact you've launched a new website, spoken on stage, sent your very first e-newsletter, or landed your first client. Raise a glass to yourself, lean into your pride, and say "I did it!" Feeling and celebration for how far we've come keeps us moving in the right direction.

4. Resource Your Feelings by Borrowing Them from the Past.

99

Resourcing involves borrowing memories and feelings that you have felt in the past, bringing those memories and physical feelings into the present, and then embodying them now to shift your mindset and emotional state. In essence, you're simply reminding your mind of what those sensations and feelings were, and letting yourself feel them again now.

Resourcing is a concept that I learned from my private coaches Carey Peters and Stacey Morgenstern of Health Coach Institute (formerly Holistic MBA) who incorporate NLP[7] principles into their work. I use this technique all the time in my own business, especially when launching a new course or stepping outside my comfort zone.

Here's the coolest part about Resourcing that utterly fascinates me:

The mind cannot tell the difference between the past and the present.

Not to get too metaphysical, but to our mind, there is only the present.

In our mind, the past is solely what we remember about events that have transpired to date, and the future has not been experienced yet. To our mind, all it knows is what we are thinking and feeling right now. The past is behind us and the future is not yet here. All we truly have is the present moment right now.

While that may be mind-boggling on the one hand, this is great news for regaining your confidence.

The confidence that you want to feel is already within you.

Because you have felt confidence previously in your life, that feeling still resides in your mind, your memory, and your body. You know exactly what it feels like to feel confident because you have felt it in the past.

Take a moment to think about something you accomplished when you felt proud of yourself. It doesn't matter what it was. What matters is that you felt confident. Maybe you:

- Got good grades in school

- Marked a milestone like a graduation or anniversary

- Hit a home run

- Love being a social butterfly and the life of the party

- Won an academic, athletic, or artistic award

- Can be whip-smart on computers

- Volunteered or did random acts of kindness for others

- Got promoted quickly at work

- Ran a marathon—or went from the couch to a 5k (or just around the block)

How confidence is expressed in the body can feel different in each person, but many people feel tall, strong, centered, grounded and relaxed. They stand with their shoulders back and straight posture. Their breathing is relaxed and they feel a sense of ease. No matter how confidence shows up for you, the goal is to raise your awareness and embody that feeling right now.

Amazingly, if you open your heart and mind and create space for confidence to emerge as it has in the past, your brain and body will respond with the same feelings now as when they originally happened.

Isn't resourcing amazing? I love it.

5. **Fake It 'Til You Make It.**

If you aren't feeling confident, it's funny how even pretending that you *do* feel confident helps your mind to move into that mindset. There's a reason we've all be taught to fake it 'til we make it.

When you pretend that you are confident, you express characteristics that others might recognize as tall, strong, or powerful even if it's the last thing you're feeling. Pretending is like acting. But even when you're acting, something shifts internally. The next thing you know, you believe it yourself and you seamlessly slip into a confident state of being.

It's not dishonest or manipulative to call in your confidence by acting confident right now. You are simply drawing on your imagination to envision yourself in a confident position instead of a fearful one. Hollywood actors do this all the time.

Think of it as trying your future self on for size. Step into the shoes of your future self by saying, feeling, and doing what your most confident self would do and see how it feels. Pretty cool, isn't it?

What's so great about pretending to be your confident future self is that, once again, your mind doesn't know the difference between the future and the present. You are tricking your mind into thinking you are confident now because you are acting that way now. It doesn't know that the future is not happening yet. Your mind responds and your mindset shifts to feel fantastic now.

6. Practice Taking Small Steps Right Out of Your Comfort Zone.

Like many other things, you get better at feeling confident the more you practice feeling confident. The more you give yourself permission to feel confident – even if you're feeling a little shaky – your entire demeanor changes. Your energy changes. You hold yourself out to the world in a different way – and the world responds accordingly.

Practice flexing your courage muscle, trying new things, taking baby steps, and give yourself permission to feel confident as you do so. Take small steps right out of your comfort zone and stretch yourself in new ways by holding your first webinar, posting your manifesto, or having your first photo shoot—even if it isn't perfect.

Remember, when it comes to business, taking baby steps matters, and done is always better than perfect.

As entrepreneurs, we need to take risks and experience discomfort—early and often.

By taking new actions and honoring your accomplishments, you are creating a pattern of action and pride so that you quickly associate taking new actions with feeling pride. It can feel wildly uncomfortable, but do it anyway. Again and again.

When you recall that you've done many new things in the past with success—even if they were tiny steps—you know you can keep taking new steps in the future.

Baby Steps That Don't Go as Planned

Sometimes, you can take baby steps—or big steps!—forward in your biz and they don't go as planned. One of the gifts of owning your own business is that you can take comfort in the fact that if your tiny action step didn't go as well as you wanted and it momentarily shook your confidence, you can quickly remedy the situation.

For example, you can always:

- Change your text on your website
- Revise your talking points for enrolling clients
- Alter the investment rate for your signature program
- Send an apology by e-mail to your distribution list
- Try a beta launch next time
- Do it differently in the future

The nature of owning your own business is that you call the shots. You can be malleable to better roll with the punches, adapt immediately, and take a different approach the next go around.

You want to do your initial research and strive to figure out what works for your clients and market, of course, but as an entrepreneur, you have no bureaucracy or hierarchy to keep you from switching gears anytime you want.

The only thing in your way is you—and you can change things anytime.

They say there's no such thing as failure in business, only feedback. There are only opportunities to tweak what you are doing or saying for the next time, the next client, the next e-newsletter, or the next live talk on stage, and to keep improving as you go.

These six techniques should give you reassurance that when you get into a confidence funk, you can quickly get out of it. Any of these techniques will shift your mindset and keep you moving forward to have the business and the life you so deeply desire.

Remember, feeling confident on the inside is key to showing confidence on the outside.

Key Takeaways from This Chapter

Having a strong inner core and balanced solar plexus chakra helps you feel confident and powerful–and even radiant!–on the outside.

Be sure to register your business at the local, state and national levels, get clear on taxes, and put your legal documents in place to watch your confidence rise. Notice how when you show up with greater self-esteem as a responsible business owner, your whole vibe shifts and you energetically uplevel from the inside out. You attract more clients who pay on time and who don't ask for refunds. You receive more income. You carry yourself with a greater sense of pride and professionalism—and the world takes notice.

Your third legal step is to file your Business Registration & Taxes.

Your third soul-centered principle is confidence.

Your third chakra that is supported and aligned is your solar plexus chakra.

Now It's Your Turn ...

Use this Legal Checklist and Business Self-Assessment to assess your core strength, regain or bolster your confidence, file your Business Registration, and get clear on Taxes.

Legal Checklist:

1. Have you found out what you need to do to register your business with your city, county, and state? (If so, you get a gold star!)

2. If you've received any income from clients or the sale of products (no matter how much), have you learned how to pay your Taxes? (If so, you get another gold star!)

3. If you haven't filed your Business Registration and dealt with Taxes yet, do you know what's holding you back?

4. Have you found an attorney and accountant who get what you do? Do you feel comfortable that they understand your industry and they'll be there to support you when you need them most?

Business Self-Assessment:

1. Do you have fears and worries that you aren't enough, that your business won't make it, and that you don't have what it takes to build your business? (If so, please don't let them stop you!)

2. Do you feel comfortable with the level of core strength you identified?

3. Do you have gut health issues, digestive problems, or sugar addiction? (Sugar and business stress often go hand in hand.)

4. Do you feel good in your core, physically, emotionally, and energetically?

5. If you can't find your confidence, which of the 6 Techniques would you like to use?

Don't forget to grab your Legal Love™ Bonus Content!

Legal Love™ Bonus Content:

"Top 10 Questions to Ask When You're Hiring an Accountant"
Free download at lisafraley.com/accountant ($197 value)

Chapter 4.

Website Terms & Conditions and Privacy Policy. Courage. Heart Chakra

My mother's side of the family is Irish Catholic. As a child, I was raised basically as a religious "mutt", but I now consider myself to be more "spiritual" than "religious." I took comparative religion courses while in college at Miami University (Ohio) because I've always been intrigued about the similarities and differences of religions of the world and the various approaches to understanding our existence on this planet—and beyond.

My love for travel has allowed me to visit some of the largest and most famous cathedrals across the globe, including in Rome, Florence, Paris, London, Moscow, St. Petersburg, Dublin, Cologne, Munich, Brussels, Ghent, New York City, and Washington, DC.

My Favorite Church in the World

Of them all, my favorite church in the entire world is Le Basilique de Sacre Coeur in Montmartre, high atop a hill in Paris.

If you aren't familiar with it, it's a gorgeous, all-white cathedral which overlooks the entire city.

In the dome of the basilica over the altar is an image of Jesus with arms outstretched surrounded by angels. The heart of Jesus is golden-yellow, and it looks as if it's illuminated from behind. The halos of the angels are also gold circles of light. The image took my breath away when I first saw it. The illuminated heart of Jesus gives the church its name—the Sacre Coeur—which translates to the "sacred heart."

The reason I love this church so much is because the heart is the center of everything – and the heart is indeed sacred. The heart is the center of our life blood in our body—literally—and our life. Having a strong heart in the physical sense, but also a big heart emotionally, is truly sacred, because it's from the heart so much flows: Love. Peace. Gratitude. Appreciation. Kindness. Compassion. Sympathy. Empathy. Respect. Admiration. Adoration. Sincerity. Passion.

And also Courage.

Courage Comes from the Heart

Having courage is non-negotiable.

Courage is critical and essential. I'd even go so far as to say that it's the most important element of a successful business. From courage and heart, all else flows.

According to etymology, the word "courage" is derived from the root "coeur," which is also the French word for "heart", so "courage" is derived from the "heart"[8].

A wide variety of spiritual teachers like Marianne Williamson and Gabrielle Bernstein, who tie their work to *A Course in Miracles* and also the Bible, teach that fear and love cannot coexist.[9] In both New Age spirituality and the Christian faith, fear can be described as merely an absence of love.[10] The idea is that having a heart-centered approach when you do, think, or say anything means you cannot simultaneously feel fear. Love and fear cannot coexist in the same moment. If you are feeling fear, then in that moment you are not choosing love.

No matter whether we look to traditional Bible passages or New Age spiritual teachers for meaning or derivation, the message is the same: if you're feeling love, you can't feel fear, and if you're feeling fear, you are forgetting to shift your mindset to love.

So often as entrepreneurs and small business owners, it's easy to get stuck forgetting to shift from fear to love. It's easy to get stuck behind fear. Stuck behind uncertainty. Stuck behind blocks. Stuck behind worry or anxiety or distress.

We're Rewarded When We Come From Service and Love, Not Fear

And yet, we are rewarded in life and in business–both financially and emotionally–when we come from service and love, not fear.

As mentioned in prior chapters, it's easy to stay stuck and hold yourself back because you're scared or not ready to move forward. I've heard so many business owners say:

- "I'm not ready."

- "I don't know enough yet."

- "I can't charge that much for my services—no one will pay that rate!"

- "Why would anyone hire me? I'm not even practicing what I preach right now."

- "I'm too new. No one even knows who I am, so why would they want to hire me?"

- "I just need to get certified first."

- "I don't have a team or a VA or the right systems in place."

- "I can't go all out right now so I just shouldn't do it at all."

But, once again, usually, that's just Fear talking. Yep, it's our Ego again—also known as our inner critic or "critter brain"—trying to keep us from exposing ourselves to risk, discomfort, judgment, failure, ridicule, exclusion, and anything else that could cause us harm. We get stuck in analysis-paralysis, indecision, procrastination, reactiveness, overindulgence, sacrifice—and the many other ways we hold back our gifts, knowledge, and truths. The Ego's main job is to keep us alive, and if it senses anything that feels remotely risky (whether it is truly life-threatening or not), it steps in to stop us cold.

So many of us worry about what people will think. We worry that if we launch our new website, it won't be "as good as" the industry leaders' websites. We worry that if we start a regular e-newsletter, no one will read it. We fear that if we create a new Facebook group, no one will join. We fear that if we take the stage, people will think we don't know what we're talking about. We worry that if we announce our newest course or offer, no one will buy it.

The Ego's fears about e-newsletters, speaking on stage, program launches, social media (and more) are usually based on old beliefs that are outdated, past programming from our childhood, or prior patterns of behaviors that kept us safe.

Our Ego would rather keep us away from dangerous situations where we might be laughed at, ignored, or disliked than to help us stretch and grow in new ways that could bring us so much more joy, connection, love, support, and income.

While the Ego may be coming from a loving intention in wanting to keep us safe and secure, the Ego is often not helpful on the journey to successful entrepreneurship because it holds us back in ways that cause suffering and pain when and where we most need to grow.

Putting legal steps in place soothes the Ego, lessens Fear and helps you to have more courage.

110

We'll dive into how to uncover your courage when you most need it, but first, we'll talk about the legal step to take that aligns with the heart chakra and courage.

As both a lawyer and an entrepreneur, I myself have felt afraid that building my business wouldn't work, that no one would want what I have to offer, and that people would think I was nuts for combining spirituality and the law. I've been afraid that my unique way of looking at the law in alignment with spirituality and the chakras would be copied by others. I've worried that I would let Fear hold me back rather than being of service to so many entrepreneurs who won't go to a lawyer because they are scared and intimidated which leaves their business vulnerable and exposed.

Lawyers and Entrepreneurs are Surprisingly Similar

You might be surprised to know that lawyers and entrepreneurs aren't all that different.

Both lawyers and entrepreneurs are tough on themselves. For some reason, both lawyers and entrepreneurs feel that we need to be perfect. We need to "do it right" and not "mess up."

We fear we may "fail" (though I don't believe there is any such thing as failure—only course-correction) or that we may never have the time, energy, money and/or freedom to have or do what we truly want.

Entrepreneurs and small business owners torture themselves with fear and doubt about what programs to create, defining their "ideal client", what offers to make, and what someone might think about their website or niche.

Likewise, lawyers torture themselves by billing thousands of hours, working long days, nights, and weekends to produce winning arguments in the courtroom and the boardroom.

Entrepreneurs worry that someone will come along and rip them off, copy their websites or steal their paid program materials, and that imposters, Copycats and Swipers, who can't seem to create their own unique copy or find their own voice will come along and profit from others' hard work.

Lawyers worry that clients will lose freedom, money, time or credibility, and that despite their research, arguments, communication and effort, the other side will win and they won't get clients the desired results.

Both entrepreneurs and lawyers fear that they will put in the work and effort and someone else will benefit.

Just as writing legal memos, drafting contracts, and writing legal briefs take tremendous effort for lawyers, creating your website and honing your message takes blood, sweat, and tears as an entrepreneur or small business owner.

So next time you meet a lawyer, remember that despite all of the negative stereotypes about lawyers, lawyers and entrepreneurs are more alike than it would appear. We aren't so different after all.

No matter what kind of a business you have, how big or small it is, whether you're a lawyer or an entrepreneur, we all worry that what we work so hard to create could vanish in an instant or that someone else will snatch away our intellectual property or work content.

It's a primal fear of loss that makes you want to protect what you birth into the world. It's important to take steps to minimize the risk of that happening.

Why Your Website is the Heart and Soul of Your Brand

If you're an online entrepreneur or a small business owner, it's likely that your website is the lifeblood of your business.

Your website is the outward facing expression of your brand. It's the most powerful place for you to show the world who you are, what you believe, what services or products you have to offer, and how you can serve others to make their life or their business better.

Your website reveals your logo, your branding, your fonts, colors, and graphics. It's an important reflection of who you are and what you stand for. It's a critical asset, and the content on your site is valuable intellectual property that belongs to you.

It can feel like being stabbed in the heart when you are surfing the web, you click on someone's site and you see that they have lifted your exact content right off of your page. Your heart starts beating quickly. You may even feel tears welling, and you feel an anger from the pit of your stomach that you didn't know existed. It's a horrible, maddening, vulnerable feeling when you see that someone else is profiting from your work without your permission.

Sadly, it happens all the time.

So often my clients come to me in tears and fury saying that someone has copied their content word for word from their home page, or ripped off several sections of their opt-in page, sales page or blog post. Once, a client even told me that someone had copied her website's about page. Seriously? Her about page? Truly, how do you copy someone's unique bio and history? Unbelievable.

Let me be clear, when someone copies or swipes your stuff, it's stealing.

Plain and simple. A Copycat may not even intend to take something of yours, but, nevertheless, when someone copies your text right off of your website, they've stolen your work.

When this happens, your Ego goes nuts. It taps right into fear and your Ego rants and raves to try to protect you: "See! I told you that you shouldn't have put that up on your site. No wonder someone copied it—it was so good and you had nothing legal on your site to protect it. Now people are going to see her website and think that I'm the one who copied her. I can't even believe that this happened."

Self-torture. The Ego can be relentless sometimes. It can shut you down, and make you want to crawl into a hole and never come out. It can stifle your voice and shut down your creativity. It can make you feel scared, angry, and defeated. It can make you even want to throw up your hands, say, "Why bother!" and close up shop. Whew!

Here's where my "Mama Lion" lawyer comes out to remind you that with strong legal documents, you can protect your work from Copycats and Swipers. Taking legal steps to protect your heartfelt creations and the heartbeat of your brand—your beloved website—can give you recourse from people who steal your work – and help you regain your courage.

You Have the Right to Protect Your Work

You have the right to protect yourself, your business, your work, and your brand.

You're allowed to be strong AND loving—without contradicting yourself.

- You're allowed to protect your work with legal documents AND have an open heart that trusts most people.

- You're allowed to have clear language in your Website Terms & Conditions that say that copying from your website is stealing and you have the right to take legal action to honor the website you worked so hard to build AND, at the same time, you can give tons of information away for free on your site.

- You're allowed to draw lines about what is your unique work product that you don't want people to copy AND what is free content that can be downloaded by others and shared from your site.

You want to be clear about what you give away for free and put boundaries around what you want to keep protected. (See, how we come back to clarity and boundaries time and time again?)

It's about respecting your work and requesting others to honor it as well.

You're allowed to have legal language on your site to keep others from treading on your creativity and benefitting from your work without your consent. Not only are you allowed to do it, but you SHOULD have Website Terms & Conditions on your site to draw your lines in the sand.

Once again, it's an "AND." It doesn't have to be an "or."

Legal Documents Don't Attract Lunatics or Lawsuits

Some clients have told me that they have been reticent to use legal documents because they don't want to create or attract "negative energy." They fear that if they put Website Terms & Conditions in place or use a Client Agreement that they're acting from a place of fear and thereby attracting unsavory situations to them.

I can understand why they might feel that way. At first glance, it's easy to assume that legal documents are cold, corporate, and salty, and therefore if you use them, you must be cold, corporate, and salty, too.

However, I believe that legal documents do not attract lawsuits or lunatics—what I lovingly call "Legal Pickles™."

To the contrary. Legal documents (especially those created with the energetic frequency and intention of Legal Love™), create clear language and boundaries to honor you, your business and your brand. They elevate your biz vibe, rather than bring it down or attract sour legal situations.

Using legal documents is the best way to honor your creativity with compassionate containers to hold your work and relationships. The intention in which your legal language is created is as powerful as the language itself that is used within them. Setting a positive intention and creating clear boundaries in writing creates nothing but positive energy that flows towards you—not negative energy.

When you take legal steps, you uplevel your professionalism, and as a result, you attract people who are comfortable with clear language and who respect others' intellectual property too.

When you feel legally safe and secure, you feel comfortable baring your heart and soul and sharing your gifts with the world. You courageously expand. You create new programs. You offer new products. You attract more clients. You make more money.

Your business explodes because you feel relaxed, safe, and secure, and you feel confident and empowered to stretch even farther towards your goals.

When you know your legal documents have your back, you feel safe to courageously expand your service to the world, and you attract people and clients who respect your work and boundaries.

Your Legal Step: Website Terms and Conditions & Privacy Policy

Let's talk about how to protect your website CONTENT.

In Chapter 1, we talked about your Website Disclaimer which is your base layer of legal protection for your website that states what you do and what you don't do, and that disclaims your liability for the information on your site. The Website Disclaimer is basically about YOU, your role, and the type of work that you do.

As you expand your basic starter website to add pages to your website, like blog posts, articles, quizzes, opt-ins, sales pages and more, the content on your website can grow exponentially. You have more creative assets, intellectual property, unique expression of ideas, and more information available for anyone to see – and to come along and copy.

Don't leave your website content vulnerable to cunning Copycats and scheming Swipers.

As you increase your website content, you need to increase your website's legal protection to keep your content safe.

There are two legal documents that you'll use to protect the actual CONTENT on your website – one to protect the words, images, and ideas that are expressed on the pages of your website, and one to protect the information that your website visitors give to you when they visit your site.

The two legal documents that protect your website content are:

1. Website Terms & Conditions – the legal document that safeguards your website copy and images from Copycats and Swipers.

2. Privacy Policy - the written policy that protects the confidentiality of the information that your website visitors give to you (it's legally required for some states and countries).

Protect Your Content with Website Terms & Conditions

Get your Website Terms & Conditions in place to protect your creative content.

Your Website Terms and Conditions help you protect your unique brand and keep it safe—including the love and care that you put into your website content, like your home page, about page, services page, opt-ins, blog posts, recipes, articles, and everything else that's on your website.

Everything that you post on your website is YOUR property (provided you haven't violated anyone else's copyright, trademark, or other intellectual property rights in sharing it on your site.)

You work hard to create your website content – to draft webpage copy, to write blog posts, to develop opt-in gifts, to schedule professional photo shoots, and to create cool images that represent the look and feel of your brand.

Your Website Terms and Conditions tells your website visitors know what they CAN—and CAN'T—do with the creative info on your site. It details which parts of the content on your site they can use for personal reasons, and which parts of your content they can't use for business or commercial purposes or in ways that earn them money, without your explicit permission.

For example, it tells website visitors that:

- They CAN download your free gift and join your tribe, but they CAN'T copy the text from your program's sales page and use it in their own business.

- They CAN link to your blog post when doing a shout out on social media, but they CAN'T take and use the images you created in Canva for your website banners.

- They CAN print off pages of your website for their personal use, but they CAN'T use any of your website copy on their own website.

It's all about using crystal-clear language that sets your boundaries so that there's no ambiguity.

Your Website Terms & Conditions tell people what you do and don't allow people to use, and stating what happens if you find that they do copy or swipe your website content. (For a free "Website Terms & Conditions Prep Sheet" to help you get clear about what content

users may use for free and what they can't use without your permission see the Legal Love™ Bonus Content at the end of this chapter.)

Your Website Terms & Conditions gives you the language and the power to enforce your ownership rights to your website content. It gives you the language you need so you can go after the Swiper to demand them to take down the pirated content or to stop using it.

People need to know that if they steal from your website or copy the words right from your webpage, you will send them a cease and desist letter to take down the information and that you reserve the right to take further legal action. It's important to have this legal language in place so that you have written backing for your argument.

Without Website Terms & Conditions, it's hard to prove that you intended to keep your content secure from Copycats. It's hard to show you weren't willingly sharing it with anyone freely.

When your website is legally naked without any legal language to address your ownership rights, you don't have an ability to make strong arguments in favor of claiming your content as yours and going after them for breach of contract terms. You don't have the legal tools you need to protect your creative content.

Protect the heart of your website and keep your copy safe.

Put robust Website Terms and Conditions in place that state in detail how website visitors can and can't use the content on your website.

Not only do you want to safeguard your own content, but you also have an obligation to keep your website visitors' information safe.

Now, let's talk about how to protect your website visitors' privacy.

Protect Your Website Visitors' Info with a Privacy Policy

You keep your website visitors' information confidential with a Privacy Policy.

You want your website visitors to know that when they visit your website and enter their name and e-mail address to sign up for your opt-in gift or to join your tribe, you will also keep THEIR personal information safe from Copycats and Swipers too.

Your Privacy Policy puts your clients and website visitors on notice that any personal details that you collect from them, including their name, e-mail address, contact information and financial information, will be kept safe and confidential, to the best of your ability.

Your Privacy Policy talks about, well, privacy—and tells people how you will use and protect their sensitive information. It also talks about their right to opt-out of your e-newsletter distribution list, that you won't spam them, that you aren't targeting children, and a whole lot more.

In some US states and other countries, you are required by law to have a Privacy Policy to protect their residents who sign up as part of your tribe.11

If you have an online business or offer an opt-in gift through your website, it's likely you're attracting visitors from all US states and abroad. Most entrepreneurs ask only for a name and e-mail address from website visitors, so you don't know where anyone is located when they sign up to receive e-newsletters or updates from you. This is totally fine, but know that you need to have a Privacy Policy in place.

If you have an opt-in box on your website or on any webpage where individuals enter their name and e-mail address, you need a Privacy Policy to comply with the law.

There are some states and countries that require that if one of their residents gives you any personal information or data (even basic info like their name and e-mail address), you must have a Privacy Policy on your website.

By the way, it doesn't matter where YOUR business is located.

Even if you as the business owner are not located in one of those states or countries yourself, having a Privacy Policy is strongly recommended so you comply with the laws of those states and countries. Undoubtedly, your list will contain at least one person from those states and countries requiring a Privacy Policy.

Not only do you follow the law when you have a Privacy Policy, but you also build trust with your website visitors. They know that you will keep their information protected, and that you won't sell it or give it to anyone else. They know that you will respect their wishes if they choose to unsubscribe from your list and that you won't spam them. They know that you have boundaries, and that you respect theirs.

You'll recall that we've discussed that when you put legal documents in place to protect yourself and your business, your frequency heightens, you create clearer boundaries and your business expands exponentially because you are taking care of your creative content and your website visitors.

When you put your Website Terms & Conditions and Privacy Policy conspicuously accessible through the footer of your website, you are taking steps to honor your own work and protect the personally identifiable information shared by your website visitors.

I believe that while you can't prevent Swipers and Copycats completely, when you put your Website Terms & Conditions and Privacy Policy in place, you create strong policies giving you practical legal language to fall back on if needed, and also clear energetic lines that cause you to attract website visitors who also respect clear boundaries.

When you honor your website and your website visitors with the right legal documents, the world responds in kind.

Courage and Your Website Terms & Conditions and Privacy Policy Align with the Heart Chakra

The heart chakra is where the three lower chakras meet the three higher chakras of the body—right at the heart of it all.

The heart chakra is located, not surprisingly, in the chest and includes the heart and the lungs. It's also associated with the thymus gland and lymphatic system. The heart chakra is represented by the color of green and is aligned with the principles of courage, tenderness, protection, devotion, respect, acceptance, forgiveness, trust and love—as well as betrayal, hurt, pain, jealousy and hatred.

This chakra is called *Anahana* in Sanskrit, which translates to "unstuck" or "unhurt." Seriously, can you believe that? It makes so much sense that the heart is the place in our energetic body where we find our courage and love to help us get "unstuck."

We'll be talking about how to find your courage when you feel scared or timid, but in the meantime, you can draw on your bravery by using this Heart Chakra Mantra:

Heart Chakra Mantra

When you are seeking more courage and love in your life or business, you can set your intention using this Heart Chakra mantra:

"I am courageous. I am valued. I am accepted. I am loved."

Putting legal protections in place to protect and support your website content and the private information that your website visitors choose to share with you is about showing tenderness, protection, respect and trust for yourself and for others. It's about:

- Tenderness—for your creative genius that you display on your website.

- Protection—of your heart's desire so that you can share it with the world.

- Respect—for your hard work, and how near and dear it is to your heart.

- Trust—for your website visitors for the information they share on your site.

Not only that, but treating your website, content, creativity and brand with love and respect is about building trust with your clients, peers, and most of all, yourself.

When we give ourselves tenderness, we gain the strength to grow.

When we protect our website content, we shift from fear and lean into courage.

When we give our website content respect, we attract fewer people who test our boundaries.

When we build trust with our website visitors, they consider us a beloved guide.

You can honor yourself, your website, and your business by protecting your creative content and intellectual property and creating a stronger energetic container to uplevel your frequency and your professionalism.

When you take legal steps, you can find the courage to follow your heart and soul and to take action steps forward toward the six- or seven-figure business that you want, rather than be paralyzed with fear and frozen in place by your Ego.

Let's explore how to find your courage when your courage seems to have vanished.

My Own Fear of Vulnerability and Visibility

I don't know about you, but as an entrepreneur, I opted to hang out my shingle, leave Corporate America, create my own businesses, and go out on my own because I wanted to be of service to the world. I tuned into my heart and my true calling, and I mustered the strength and courage to set out on my own—not backed by a big law firm or organization—to deliver heart-felt services, programs, and products to the world.

I became a heart-centered business owner who wanted to make a difference in people's lives and support them as they take steps in their business or life towards what they really want.

But in the daily business of being a small business owner or entrepreneur, it's easy to slide back into feeling fearful. It's easy to forget that we are moved by a strong sense of service when we're terrified to send our first e-newsletter, share our first free e-course, offer a paid course, take the stage for a speaking gig, or share our professional photos on our newly-designed website. It's easy to choose fear instead of love, and let it stop us from showing up in bigger ways in service for the world.

At least it was for me. Even though some would say I am a "successful" lawyer, I have been paralyzed by fear which kept me from getting bigger and shining brighter.

As I've shared, I myself lived in a full-out state of fear and was scared out of my mind to share my desire to bring more spirituality into how I speak about the law for the first two years of my business. Here are a few examples as to how I've played small in my biz:

I was scared to send e-newsletters because I feared people wouldn't want to hear what I had to say so I didn't write them regularly until 18 months after I started my business—18 months!

I had a professional photo shoot with a top photographer in a studio on Venice Beach used by movie stars and rock bands—and I didn't show anyone (other than my husband and a few close friends) the photos for months after I got them.

I was terrified to film videos for my legal course. While I love speaking on stage in front of large and small audiences, and I've spoken at live events around the world, it took me months to muster the courage to appear on video. I couldn't understand why videos felt so scary for me when:

- I've spoken on a large stage at an industry conference in front of hundreds of lawyers talking about electronic medical records and patient confidentiality—and let me tell you, lawyers are a tough crowd!

- I've spoken on stage at a national conference in front of 1,000 attendees, and I have spoken at smaller, more intimate events ranging from 20 to 300.

- I am videotaped giving speeches on stage and that camera doesn't bother me at all.

- I feel like my natural, enthusiastic self while speaking on stage with an audience present, where both the audience and I can exchange energy and feel energized and engaged.

Yet, to me, filming videos was utterly panic-inducing. I tried to make it fun by filming videos wearing different dresses in the colors of the chakras while I explained how each legal document is aligned with a chakra. I love sharing my unique legal philosophy and was excited about wearing chakra-colored dresses, but recording the videos felt really scary.

The 4 Steps that Made Me Feel Safe to Film Videos

I could only muster my courage after I had taken these four steps to make myself feel as safe and comfortable as possible:

1. **I set up a video studio in my basement.** I went downstairs on a Saturday, moved a bunch of boxes, and cleared out space to film videos in my basement next to my infra-red sauna. I bought everything I needed to get me started: six professional lights, white and green backdrops, two tripods (one for the camera and one for the iPad with a teleprompter app), a portable microphone, a Macbook Pro, and the iMovie app so my team could edit the videos afterwards. I needed to get all of the video gear ready to soothe my "critter" brain around my technology worries.

2. **I hired a stylist to help me pick out my wardrobe.** My dear friend and amazing stylist Carrie Montgomery helped me select nine dresses—seven that were in the respective colors that I was using for chakras (red, orange, yellow, green, turquoise, blue, indigo, violet), one for the welcome video (hot pink) and one for the promotional videos for the opt-in calls (black and white). I had no idea what style of dress would look good on film, so having Carrie help me with each outfit made me feel more confident about my appearance and reduced my fears.

3. **I hired a video coach/set director/makeup artist to help me before, during, and after the shoot.** Not only is Carrie a stylist, but, lucky for me, she also went to film school. Carrie came to my house to put on my makeup, design the video set, and help me feel more secure on camera. She coached me how to stand, speak and gesture, and she filmed the nine videos with the proper lighting and set. Having her coach and encourage me on set was essential. (I honestly couldn't have done it without her!)

4. **I worked with a spiritual advisor AND a one-to-one business coach to work through my blocks.** I knew I was terrified to use my voice and appear on video, but I didn't understand why. I confirmed through two different spiritual readings (a separate past-life

regression and an Akashic record reading) that I may have been killed in a past lifetime for publicly sharing my opinions by being burned to death on a platform in the town square with townspeople cheering and laughing. Though it may sound completely crazy (believe me, it did to me too, at first!), the idea of being killed for expressing controversial views deeply resonated with me on a cellular level, and I wouldn't be surprised if it had happened in some prior lifetime. Uncovering this possibility put me at ease – as strange as it sounded - because it helped my Ego to work through the blocks and stand in the video spotlight knowing there may be some underlying spiritual reason for my fears. (Though we may never know the truth as to whether it happened, the hypothesis alone was helpful to me.)

It took all of this effort to film ten 90-second videos for my business, something that many people can do simply by whipping out a cell phone, pressing the "record" button, and talking into the camera. For me, filming those videos was a monumental accomplishment.

And, in case you're wondering, those first videos weren't ideal. We did a bazillion takes. I was stilted and stiff, and my gestures were awkward. My voice wavered and I talked too quickly. I was clearly, visibly uncomfortable on film. I felt visible and I felt vulnerable. It felt so unnatural, and I hated every minute of it. Six months later, Carrie came over again and we re-shot every single video—and then a few months later, we even re-shot them again.

I looked a wee bit more comfortable on camera each round of takes, purely because I knew what to expect the more times we did it, but anyone who knows me can tell I was nervous. I've fully acknowledged my fear of speaking with a camera in my face and my utter vulnerability in using this type of media. I totally own all of it—and I gave a big hug to that scared part of me who dug deep to muster her courage to keep recording videos anyway. I knew the only way to get better doing them was to keep doing them.

Even today, my videos aren't my proudest work, but they look professional and they get the job done – and they are MUCH better now than my first go-around.

Here's the important part of the story: Despite my fear, I found my courage and I did it anyway.

Without becoming aware of what was holding me back, I would've stayed captive in a fear-based state designed to keep me motionless. When Fear runs the show, we let uncertainty, confusion, our outdated beliefs about ourselves or the world, our inability to make decisions, crazy rationalizations about why it's unsafe to proceed, anxiety, panic, sleeplessness, avoidance, distractions, and unhealthy habits rule our lives and our business—and stand in the way of everything we want. It's exhausting just thinking about it, isn't it?

We can't stay immersed in Fear or it will have its way with us.

Don't Try to Remove Fear: Just Go Around It.

When it comes to Fear, I've discovered that shifting the way I think about Fear lessens its hold over me. We so often forget that Fear is relative. It only needs to be as big or as small as we let it be.

The goal isn't to remove Fear altogether.

It's not about annihilating uncertainty and plowing through trepidation. It's not possible or even desirable to completely remove Fear. As we've discussed in prior chapters, Fear is engrained in our neurological wiring as human beings so that we can survive. We can't make Fear disappear entirely—that's for sure—nor should we. Pushing and shoving and trying to eliminate fear doesn't work. It's wasted energy. Fear is one of our human emotions that joins the countless others and comes along for the ride through our entire life.

We'll fool ourselves if we think we can eliminate the Fear we feel.

The trick is to find your way over, around, and through it so you can keep taking action steps to fuel and grow your business, even if you're terrified to film videos just like I was. Rather than try to yank yourself out of the muck, deny Fear or squish it down, it's easier to acknowledge Fear and flow with it, rather than push against it. It's easier to embrace that you're scared and do what you need to do to surround yourself with whatever you need to feel safe.

In my case, when I purchased video equipment, got the emotional support, and took every action I could think of to feel safe—all the way down to selecting colorful dresses and the shade of lipstick to wear— it wasn't that I was trying to make the Fear go away. Rather, I was honoring the Fear by making myself feel as comfortable as possible in a very uncomfortable setting so I could go forward, EVEN THOUGH I felt so much Fear. I felt scared AND I did it anyway.

Once again, it's an "AND" – not an "OR."

Unless we listen to our Fear, acknowledge it, honor it and work with it, it stays big and out of control. But once we recognize it, give it our attention, soothe it, and not make it "wrong," we're able to lessen its death grip on us. We can allow Fear to exist as a background voice in our head, no longer holding a microphone (or a megaphone!) and serving as the lead vocalist in our mind. We find the courage to grab the mike and make Fear a backup singer.

But what about those days when Fear is screaming with a megaphone and you can't seem to find your courage?

How to Find Your Courage When You're Really, Really Scared

Sometimes, we can't seem to embrace the Fear. Its grip is too tight and we can't find our bravery. What's a biz owner to do then?

Using these 6 Steps for Taming Your Fear and Uncovering Your Courage to Move Forward can help when you can't find your fear and you need to uncover your courage.

---

6 Steps for Taming Your Fear and Uncovering Your Hidden Courage

1. **Remember that Fear is a façade.** Fear is like the Wizard in *The Wizard of Oz* before the curtain was pulled back to reveal an old man in a green coat creating a false reality with a bunch of gadgets and smoke machines. Having a visual representation of Fear as a little old man at the end of the Yellow Brick Road helps to separate the Fear from you—because you are not your Fear. Remember, Fear is just a smokescreen.

2. **Choose courage**. When your Ego is raising its voice remember your Ego draws on your old conditioning, patterning, stories, beliefs and practices that kept you alive in the past and uses them to try to keep you safe now. When you understand that the Ego is aligned with the past and courage is aligned with your future, you can choose to align your thoughts and energy with your courage, not your Fear.

3. **Be gentle with yourself.** When you're afraid, have compassion for the part of you that's scared. Be gentle with yourself, like you would with a child who is afraid of the monster under the bed. Don't beat yourself up for being scared. Extend kindness, like you would to a friend or client who was hurting, and be gentle, kind, and loving with yourself.

---

4. **Give yourself permission.** Give yourself permission to not be perfect, to look and feel uncomfortable, to give it your best shot and remember that "done is better than perfect." Remember me and my video experience. Cut yourself some slack and just do it.

5. **Get support.** Get the support that you need to move forward. Invest in yourself and your business to do it. Hire a video coach. Buy the equipment. Find a stylist. Support yourself with coaches and spiritual healers. When you get the training, education, certification, equipment, processes, and structure you need to do what scares you, you can stretch yourself to grow. Get exactly what you need so you can get out of your own way.

6. **Take baby steps.** Take the tiniest baby step towards what you want. You WILL be scared. You WILL feel nervous. You WILL feel uncomfortable. If it's new, it's part of the deal. Feel the fear and do it anyway—even in small, baby steps. Because when you take just one small step, it opens the door to the next step … and the next...and the next.

Courage (Like Crow Pose) Improves with Practice

Courage is like a muscle. It needs to be flexed.

Flexing your courage muscle is a lot like working out. In fact, it's a lot like trying to do crow pose in yoga class for the first time. Learning how to balance on your hands while propping your bent knees on top of your elbows can feel intimidating and tricky, especially in front of a class full of yoga students who've been doing it for years.

Courage mastery is gained through incremental steps.

To master your crow pose, you start with bringing up one knee onto an elbow and shifting your weight forward. You'll probably wobble a bit, then add the second knee, learn to balance and the next thing you know you're in full-fledged crow pose. Even if you're not so good at it at first, it's okay. What's important is to try. Get out of your comfort zone.

Just like crow pose, your effort may look messy, lopsided, and uncomfortable, and you may feel like you're going to topple forward onto your face at any time, but when you keep taking small steps to improve, you'll get more courageous with every attempt and you'll get better and better each time.

As we've discussed, you can't plow through Fear when it comes to life or business, but when you take any of the 6 Steps to Taming Your Fear and Aligning with Your Courage to Move Forward, you can tame your Fear by embracing it and loving it, so that you don't get stuck and frozen right where you are.

Your courage is there waiting for you to flex it. You've drawn on it countless times throughout your life, and it's waiting for you to draw on it whenever you want. By starting a business and picking up this book to learn what legal steps you need as you grow, you've tapped into your deep well of courage already.

Remember that right now, in this very moment, your courage is accessible within you. It hasn't really gone anywhere. Right here, right now, you are full of courage – even if you can't see it.

You are deeply courageous right now.

Each time when you step out into the great unknown, adjust your mindset and get out of your head and into your heart, you are consciously choosing to be courageous. Remind yourself that you're creating videos or launching a new course because you're coming from a place of service and deeply wanting to make a positive difference in other people's lives. That deep yearning to help others alone should motivate you to flex your courage muscle and take the risk.

Why It's Worth the Risk

For me, when I feel scared, it helps to remember that if my work reaches even one person who is searching for help and the very expertise I can offer, then it's worth the risk of looking crappy on camera, or being ridiculed, judged, ignored, or embarrassed.

You hear a lot of people say this and wonder if they truly mean it, but I do.

When I settle into my heart and come from a place of love regarding anything that I create and I shift my mindset into a warm, loving, caring feeling of being of service, then I can move the Fear aside and do it—even if it's not going to be perfect or polished, or if I appear stilted or stiff or unnatural on film.

My "come from" is to be of service so that other business owners, coaches, and entrepreneurs can have the beautiful lives and businesses they've dreamed of—without staying mired in fear, worry, and doubt because they're legally naked.

Helping people with Legal Love™ is more important to me than my Fear.

I've noticed when I create a new do-it-yourself legal template or self-study legal course from my heart to be of service to others—and not from a place of fear, lack, scarcity or need—my whole energy shifts towards the positive, and I raise my energetic frequency to call in and attract clients who are happy to pay me and eager to be supported.

The same is true for any of us. When we tune into our hearts, get into the flow, shift into being of service, draw on our courage, and work with our Fear and "do it anyway," we shift our entire vibe and draw in more clients, income, friends and supporters.

When you come from your heart, you find your courage.

And when you feel safe and secure with a strong legal foundation for your business, you feel even more courageous.

Key Takeaways from This Chapter

As you think about the next steps for your business and the legal documents you want to put in place, remember to take a moment to sidestep your Fear and choose love. Put your Website Terms & Conditions and Privacy Policy in place to protect your work and safeguard others' content. Consciously choose courage. Choose your heartfelt work, your creativity, and your dreams. Choose to feel the Fear—and choose to take action anyway.

Your fourth legal step is to create your Website Terms & Conditions and Privacy Policy.

Your fourth soul-centered principle is Courage.

Your fourth chakra that is supported and aligned is your heart chakra.

Now It's Your Turn ...

Use this Legal Checklist and Business Self-Assessment to sidestep your Fear, find your Courage, protect your website content, and safeguard the privacy of your visitors' information with your Website Terms & Conditions and Privacy Policy.

Legal Checklist:

1. Do you have a website that contains a lot of content you've poured your blood, sweat, tears and pocketbook into?

2. Do you have your Website Terms & Conditions on your site to protect your content? (If so, you get a gold star!)

3. Do you have an opt-in gift or an invitation to join your e-newsletter community where you collect names, e-mail addresses, or other information from visitors to your site?

4. Do you have your Privacy Policy in place? (If so, you get another gold star!)

Business Self-Assessment:

1. Who are you here to serve? How do you serve them? What's unique or extra-special about the service you provide?

2. How do you love up your clients? What do you do to show that you value and love the people who are drawn to you?

3. Where do you feel vulnerable in your business? What steps can you take to get the support, information, equipment, or skills that you need to feel ready to take that step—even if it won't be polished or perfect (like my videos)?

4. Why is it worth the risk to you to have your business? To do what you love? To take an action step that's been scaring you? What makes it worth it?

5. What fear do you need to step around? Which of 6 Techniques for Taming Your Fear and Aligning with Your Courage to Move Forward can you try out?

Don't forget to grab your Legal Love™ Bonus Content!

Legal Love™ Bonus Content:

"Website Terms & Conditions Prep Sheet" to get clear about what content users may use for free and what they can't use without your permission.

Free download at lisafraley.com/websitetermsprepsheet. ($197 value)

Chapter 5.

Terms of Use for Online Programs & Products. Communication. Throat Chakra.

In high school and college, I was a straight A student (except for Organic Chemistry, which I bombed). I was active in clubs and sports and cheerleading. I was in the Honor Society and was a Miami University Scholar-Leader. I was everything from president of the Youth in Government Club to president of my sorority pledge class in college to president of the Junior League as an adult.

I was the oldest child in the family. I was the leader. I was the responsible one.

My younger sister is smart and talented too, but somehow she got away with a lot more than I did. She didn't seem to be as burdened by a sense of "responsibility" the same way I did as the oldest child. I was the one who felt I had to do everything right.

It's not by coincidence that my Type-A personality led me right from college to law school, and to amazing opportunities like an internship on Capitol Hill and being offered a job in the White House (that I foolishly declined to go to law school instead). It's not by chance that I worked at a large, prestigious law firm, ran three marathons, and was named one of Business First's "Forty Under 40" in Columbus, Ohio when I was just 29.

I was a go-getter. I was an achiever. I wanted an "A" in everything I did. I was a people-pleaser.

I'm the "Good Girl"

I've always been a "good girl" – or felt I needed to be.

I was always trying to do what was expected of me—whether to get top grades, a great job, or praise-filled accolades—so it made it hard for me to do anything that felt "out of the box."

For decades, I didn't even feel like I was allowed to leave the box. Not because my parents or anyone else imposed that on me, but because I had decided long ago that I deeply valued having a secure job, planned income, and professional recognition.

Not surprisingly, all of that achieving and people-pleasing made it hard for me to fully express myself.

It never dawned on me that I might feel freer and more secure by setting my own schedule, achieving my own goals, and working for myself.

I honestly didn't know that I wasn't meant to thrive outside of the box until I left the box of the nine-to-five corporate world. I had nothing to compare it to, so I didn't know what it felt like to do anything but to work for someone else.

I'm still an over-achiever, so admittedly, I still work way too many hours holed up in my home office (just ask my husband!), but it's for my own business, which makes a huge difference. I get to decide when I choose to work and when I choose to play. I get to work with my own team, and I set my own hours.

But for a while I needed a lot of permission to look at the world from the perspective of outside of the "box."

I Needed Permission

I needed permission to call myself part lawyer, part coach and part spiritual soul sister.

I needed permission to charge for my services and receive payment for my work in my own business without being backed by a big law firm or organization.

I needed permission to speak my truth and talk about the law, chakras, and energy in a way that is not typical for a lawyer.

I needed permission to do what my heart wanted me to do—and to stop doing what I was "supposed" to be doing by working in a law firm or other respected, established institutions.

I'm not going to lie: I was a nervous wreck when I first stepped out of the box. I even stayed in my day job for 18 months as I built my business up on the side because it was too frightening to leap all at once from a stable day job to uncertain business ownership. Utterly terrifying.

I built my business as what my former business coach, Carey Peters, calls a "slow burn," taking one baby step at a time. I started by talking only with my clients and dear friends about how I aligned legal steps with the chakras, because it felt too vulnerable to speak openly about my views. It took me two full years to really own it, and it was the positive support of the open-minded, entrepreneurial community of health coaches, business coaches, B-Schoolers, spiritual healers, creative artists and designers who gave me the confidence to more openly share my perspective and message.

Using your voice and speaking your truth about what you feel or how you see the world can feel foreign if you're not used to doing it.

You may worry that people will:

- Not like you

- Not understand you or your ideas

- Harm your reputation on social media

- Question your credentials and experience

- Claim you are a fraud or that you're doing something wrong

- Belittle you, ridicule you, and exclude you somehow

- Come after you to hurt you or your property

Gulp. That's a lot to be afraid of. I have feared most of the things on this list myself at times.

If we're being honest with ourselves, most of us who believe, live or work outside of the traditional "box" have experienced these same fears.

I know first-hand that it can feel scary to stand up and say, "This is what I believe," and declare my values, truths, philosophy, knowledge, experience, expertise, and identity. Very scary.

If you are anything like me, you may need permission to speak your truth too.

You may need permission to let go of:

- Other people's expectations of you

- Your own expectations of what you think you are supposed to do

- Others' opinions of you

- Feeling responsible all the time

- Feeling like you are not allowed to rock the boat

- Censoring yourself so you won't upset someone

- Playing small and avoiding the spotlight

You certainly don't need MY permission to do any of these things.

You only need your own permission. But if you are like me, you may want someone to tell you that it's okay—the same way that I needed my own coaches to support and encourage me along the way. If that's you, and you would like permission, then I give you my full approval.

I Give You Permission

I give you permission to stand in your truth, own who you are, and say what you believe, without apology or explanation. You have a unique voice, and we're eager to receive what you'd like to share. We want you to show up, play big and shine. We are counting on you to step up.

It can feel scary to bare your heart and soul to the world. It can feel a little exciting – and a little unnerving – at first.

But, as you speak your truth and spread your message farther and wider, you establish yourself as a legitimate and serious player in the marketplace. People take notice of how you run your business, how you present your brand, and how generous you are with your clients.

As you expand your message, it's inevitable that you'll become bigger, bolder, and braver.

When you raise your professionalism and communicate to the world that you should be taken seriously as a biz owner—because you take yourself more seriously. You'll begin to reach more people. Your launches will expand, your sales will go up, and you'll receive more income.

When you use legal documents to support your expanding services, group programs, and online programs, you not only show the world your level of professionalism, but you protect your work and safeguard your ideas.

Stepping up and spreading your message more visibly can feel daunting at first, especially if you've created a successful group program, product, or online course. You may realize that the more people who see and purchase your work, the more you risk that someone may try to copy or use it in their own businesses without your permission. This can be worrisome, and rightly so.

But there are steps you can take to legally protect your work and to feel more comfortable communicating a wider message. We'll tackle the legal part first, and then talk about the business angle.

Your Legal Step: Terms of Use for Online Programs and Products

When you expand your message, many online entrepreneurs move from one-on-one services to group offers to serve more people at once. You may develop a group program or online course. You may offer a digital product or sell a physical product through your website. You may write books or e-books, or create audio or video courses.

When you move from serving one to serving many, or widening your reach of customers through your website, you'll need different legal language to protect your work sold in paid courses, programs or products. (Remember that for one-to-one programs with clients you'll use a Client Agreement from Chapter 2, but for everything else you sell through your website, you'll use this legal step.)

The legal document you'll need is called Terms of Use - which can also be called Terms of Service, Purchase Terms, or Terms & Conditions.

Because there are so many different names for legal terms, I like to call them "Terms of Use for Online Programs and Products" (or "Terms of Use" for ease and clarity,) because they explain how others can USE the programs and products that you sell online.

Your Terms of Use are Your Sales Policies

Your Terms of Use are your SALES POLICIES to protect your group programs, online courses and other products you sell through your website.

Your Terms of Use are designed to protect any creative content sold through your website that's not a one-on-one service, like your:

- Group programs

- Online courses

- Downloadable info products

- Video modules

- Audio recordings

- E-books

- Physical products

- And more!

Your Terms of Use are the sales terms that your purchasers agree to before they click on your "buy now" button or enter their credit card information when they are shopping on your site.

Note that the Terms of Use are different from the Website Terms & Conditions addressed in Chapter 4. You'll remember that the Website Terms & Conditions protect your actual website content—like your home page, sales page, about page and blog posts.

By contrast, your Terms of Use are sales terms for your PAID programs and products—like your group programs, online video courses, e-books, downloadable digital products, or tangible physical products that you sell through or on your website.

Terms of Use contain your liability disclaimers, online commerce policies, payment and refund policies, intellectual property guidelines, communications guidelines, and other details related specifically to the purchase. They also contain specific policies related to how the content or product may be used by the consumer.

Protect Your Income & Practically
"Refund-Proof" What You Sell

Terms of Use protect your income and practically "refund-proof" what you sell online.

For anything that you sell online, you'll want to be sure you spell out your clear and robust payment terms and refund policy. If you sell tangible products, like gluten-free bars or yoga DVDs, you'll also want to include your shipping, exchange, return and refund policies for physical goods.

Because these Terms of Use are designed for the sale of goods and services, you'll want to link them to your SALES PAGES and ONLINE SHOPPING CART. You put them on your sales page or shopping cart so purchasers can see them when they are buying your course or product.

(You don't want to post them on your website. As you learned in prior chapters, you'll post your Website Disclaimer, Website Terms & Conditions and Privacy Policy through the footer of your website, but your Terms of Use are posted on your sales page or online shopping cart – not in the footer of your site.)

3 Big Reasons You Need Terms of Use

Your Terms of Use contain contractual language that purchasers voluntarily agree to when they buy your program or course. If you can't tell yet, that's an enormous reason why you need to have Terms of Use in place. There are also a few other key reasons to have Terms of Use:

1. **To provide your sales policies and program rules.**

You want to spell out your sales policies, so your purchasers are clear about your boundaries, and you have a positive working relationship right from the start. Terms of Use are contractual terms between you and the purchaser. They are written terms containing all of your policies related to the purchase and use of your paid offering.

You want your Terms of Use to cover areas like:

- Intellectual Property Rights, so they know what they can and can't do with your content

- Online Commerce and Payment policies

- Refund Policy and Chargeback rules

- Participant Conduct and Community guidelines

- Lots of Disclaimers, including Medical, Legal, Technology and more

- No Guarantees Clause

- Limitations on Liability and Release of Claims

- Expectations about group interaction (if your program or offer includes support in a Facebook group, website or online community)

- And so much more (I told you it was a hefty document!)

You want purchasers to "check the box" to show that they agree to the terms and understand to everything you request of them—BEFORE they complete their purchase. Whether or not you have a checkbox (also called a tickbox) on your sales page or shopping cart, you want to get their agreement to your terms BEFORE they enter their credit card information.

Do I Have to Use a Checkbox?

The purpose of using the checkbox to get purchasers to agree to your Terms of Use is to prove that they saw the terms – even if they didn't read them.

Using a checkbox is not legally required. It's the gold standard because purchasers are taking an affirmative action to indicate that they agreed to your terms, but it's not required.

Before they click the "buy now" button or type their credit card information into your shopping cart, you want them to agree that, "By purchasing this program, you agree to these Terms of Use" and you want to make your Terms of Use visible to your purchaser before they commit to the purchase.

It's hard for a purchaser to deny that they had access to the terms when they physically clicked the checkbox that they agreed to the Terms of Use. It's hard for them to later disagree with the terms because they agreed to them up front.

Using a checkbox is a way to give you added protection that you aren't hiding your policies or not making them available before a purchase is made, and thus, makes it harder for a purchaser to argue that they didn't agree to them at the outset.

2. **To have strong legal language to fall back on.**

A second reason to have Terms of Use is to have written policies all in one place where purchasers can see them.

You want clear, robust, and meaty sections in your Terms of Use that reduce ambiguity and spell out where you draw lines so you have strong legal language to support you in the event of a conflict. If you don't put your policies for your PAID programs and courses in writing, it's hard to prove where you draw your boundaries. For example:

- When you have no written language to fall back on, it's difficult to show that you intended to allow your purchasers to learn and grow

145

from use of your program, course or product, but you don't want them to use your content in their own offers or businesses.

- When you don't have anything in writing and a purchaser wants their money back, you'll struggle to resolve the conflict in your favor because you can't prove that they agreed to your "no refund" policy.

- When you don't have your terms clearly stated and someone uses your content in a new course they are creating, it's hard to show that you had rules that didn't allow them to use your course content for anything other than their own personal use.

What Happens If Purchasers Don't Read Them?

Even if purchasers don't read your Terms of Use, they're still required to follow them.

Putting your terms in writing makes them transparent so your purchasers know where you stand.

Even if they tick the box without reading the Terms of Use, the purchaser made an empowered choice whether to read them or not. And while they may not always (or rarely!) be read, your Terms of Use share your policies in a clear way and ultimately protect you and your work, and you have them to fall back on if needed.

Regardless of whether the purchaser has read the Terms of Use thoroughly, glanced at them for two seconds, or didn't bother to look at them at all, they are still legally bound by them.

That checkmark indicates that they chose to agree with them. And even if you don't have a checkbox, they are still required to follow them by virtue of the fact they purchased your program or product online.

You cover two bases when you have written Terms of Use: You inform your purchasers of your policies and you protect your work.

The more you create strong, clear expectations and guidelines about the use of your work, the tighter your legal and energetic boundaries will be. This likely will result in more income, fewer Copycats and Swipers, reduced refunds, and less stress for you.

3. To protect your intellectual property from Copycats and Swipers.

The biggest reason to use Terms of Use is to have legal language to support you if someone steals or copies your work.

One of the biggest worries business owners have is that someone will come along and steal or swipe your programs, courses, or products that you sell online.

If any of these scenarios have happened to you, you know it feels like crap:

- A friend tells you that she was browsing online and another coach swiped your exact program copy and inserted into her new course.

- One of your group program participants decides she wants to quit halfway through, and she just stops paying you by removing her credit card on file.

- An online course client knows you have a no-refund policy, but she decides she doesn't like the course content, so she issues a chargeback through her credit company.

Sadly, these things happen all the time. Terms of Use back you up if they do.

Terms of Use allow you to clearly claim ownership to your programs and products and put others on notice. In the Terms of Use, you can state what content you are giving your purchasers a limited license to use and for what purpose they can specifically use it.

Terms of Use spell out what someone can or can't do with your intellectual property and your original content. For an online course, you want the language to be very clear and thorough in saying "this is what you can do with my course content" and "this is what you cannot do with my course content" so you protect your work. For a physical product, you want to be clear about how to safely use your product and provide any product warnings or instructions.

For example, you want to clearly draw your lines that:

- Course registrants can't copy your downloadable information or products and insert the language and images from your program guide into THEIR program guide for their new offer.

- Video course purchasers can't swipe your video copy and insert it into THEIR video or audio course.

- Group program participants can't transcribe your recorded group calls and offer them as a bonus in THEIR course without your permission.

- Product purchasers can't return the product if it's opened or after 30 days – or whatever your refund policy allows.

Just like a Client Agreement creates boundaries and clarity with a one-on-one client, Terms of Use draw your lines and state your expectations for your group program, online course or product purchasers.

Without Terms of Use, you have no legal language to fall back on to show you have claimed your ownership rights and established guidelines for use of your online programs or products.

You need your purchasers to agree to your Terms of Use so you can go after them if they snag your stuff without permission.

It's your choice how your work and products are used by others; it's not their right to come take them without your permission. Yet, it's your responsibility as the business owner to be clear and direct, and to have the right legal language and intellectual property protections in place to claim the work that you worked so freaking hard to create.

Longer Is Better

Okay, before your mind ends up in the gutter, I'm talking about legal documents here, not, ahem … other things.

Terms of Use are usually comprehensive, which means that generally they are very long. Remember, as I've said in a prior chapter: "When it comes to the law, less is not more. More is more." This is why legal documents are often lengthy. If you don't say it, it's hard to prove that you meant it.

When it comes to relationships, we often have the most tenuous relationship with people who are buying a course or product without much, if any, one-on-one interaction with you. Because you haven't built a tight one-on-one relationship, they may not feel as much of a sense of loyalty or obligation to honor you or your work. No judgment about that, of course. Just an observation based on my own experience.

The more one-on-one interaction your purchaser has with you, the more loyalty. The more tenuous the relationship, the more copying and stealing that occurs.

How to Handle Copycats and Swipers

When someone comes along and swipes or copies your work, you are put in an uncomfortable jam. While you may fuming inside, believe it or not, there are times when Copycats and Swipers take and use your work without ill intent.

Copycats are often just TRYING to be you—or be like you—or have what you have—because they don't have a clear vision of what they want to create or do for themselves yet. People who take from you may do so simply because they're at a loss, and your program or course content conveniently suits what they need. They most likely aren't trying to hurt you or knowingly steal your stuff; they're just can't find their own voice to develop their own.

Sometimes Copycats and Swipers don't even intend to use your content verbatim or steal your ideas. They may have been checking out your website or course offering looking for "inspiration", and they next thing they know they're copying your content word for word. It's common for newer entrepreneurs to look to others' work as an example and model their sales pages and course content after them, because they haven't figured out how to create a course or teach a program that authentically comes from their own heart and soul.

When this happens, you are entitled to feel angry and offended. You are allowed to believe they are inauthentic and underhanded. You can tell them to stop using your work. You are correct in that you have legal rights and remedies.

But, I invite you to presume innocence first.

Presume Innocence First

You already know that I'm not your typical lawyer. I favor Legal Love™ over litigation, so it likely won't come as a surprise when I say to "presume innocence first" if you think someone's swiped your copy.

Check out this situation: I had two clients who are complete opposite of each other. Both are heart-centered, but one is a business coach with a straight-talk, no-nonsense approach to coaching, and the other is a spiritual healer who uses astrology, numerology, and crystals when working with clients. They both came up with the EXACT SAME NAME for their online program. I couldn't believe it when I heard it.

The name was so unique that if they had seen each other's sales pages, they would have easily concluded in one second flat that the other was a Copycat. But they weren't. I knew they didn't know each other. They didn't belong to the same social media groups. They didn't have the same clients. They were at opposite ends of the political spectrum.

Other than the fact they both are caring coaches and healers who are loving people and talented professionals, they likely had no way of knowing what the other was doing. It was unbelievable.

Because I value client confidentiality, I did not reveal to either of them that I knew that they both had come up with the same online course name. Until one of them had gotten a trademark or copyright, both could use the name freely (presuming it didn't infringe on any existing intellectual rights of others).

This is the perfect example as to why it's wise to not jump to conclusions if you think someone has stolen your stuff, especially if they haven't been a client or someone who has been exposed to your work.

> That person certainly may have copied you—but you both also may have been divinely and magically inspired at the same time. I know for a fact, it can happen.

Having your work copied without your consent can feel like a violation and can simultaneously make you feel furious, frustrated, and frenetic. You can feel victimized and helpless and sad, and not know what to do when it happens or how to prevent it in the future.

When a Copycat or Swiper doesn't treat your program or product with respect and compassion, I do believe that karma will even the playing field at some point. Someone will come and snag THEIR stuff at some point, or bite them in the behind when they aren't looking. Somehow it always evens out in divine timing. What goes around always comes around. The Copycat or Swiper may appear to be successful for a while, but inevitably they'll come crashing down because they've built a shell of a business on the core of someone else's. They've built a house of cards, and that never lasts.

But even if you believe they'll surely suffer from their sins later, what about now?

When Copycats copy your program content or Swipers snag your course copy, you do have recourse, especially if the Copycat or Swiper agreed to your Terms of Use upon purchase. That's why having Terms of Use are so important.

Provided your Terms contain clear language about what happens if they use your content without permission, you have legal rights that you can enforce.

What to Do if Someone Swipes Your Stuff

If you think that someone has swiped your stuff, take a few deep breaths, wipe the tears from your eyes, and feel empowered that you have options. I know it feels crappy to discover your work has been snatched, but draw on your inner Mama (or Papa!) Lion and take the following three steps:

1. Take Screenshots of Everything

Your first step is to take screenshots of everything. Everything and anything that you believe is copied from your website, sales page, program guide, video course, product packaging—and more. Take screenshots and put them in a folder with a label where you can easily find them later. These screenshots will be important evidence to support your position.

2. Presume Innocence First (See above box.)

Your second step is to consider for a moment that the swiping wasn't intentional. You can reach out with a friendly e-mail and say something like, "Hey, I was checking out your site today, and you may not even realize it, but I noticed that you use language that is exactly the same as [or substantially similar to] the copy on my sales page. I'm curious as to how and when you created your site page and if you could tell me more about it." Start with curiosity and kindness first. Start by treating others the way you would wish to be treated – with love.

3. Send a Cease and Desist Letter

If your friendly e-mail goes unacknowledged or you get a nasty reply in return (some people can be so unkind), then send a "cease and desist" letter asking them to stop using your content. Be specific and clear about what you believe was stolen or copied and state specifically how and when you'd like them to "cease" using your content and the date they need to "desist" from further use. (To obtain a free "Cease and Desist Letter" template, see the Legal Love™ Bonus Content at the end of this chapter.)

4. Talk with a Local Attorney.

If you receive no response—or yet another unpleasant one—talk with an attorney in your state who can advise you as to the best course of action. You may want the attorney to send a letter on your behalf. You may want to file a lawsuit in small claims court or another court, depending on the situation. If you have Terms of Use in place (which you should!), it may contain an alternative dispute resolution clause and state that any conflict will be decided by mediation or arbitration. Your attorney can help you assess the right approach based on the time, money, and damage involved.

Most importantly, know that you are not helpless. You have rights and you can enforce them if you wish to do so.

Part of claiming your work is using your voice to say that your work has value – and your Terms of Use helps you do that.

When you share your work in a bigger way from a place of love and service, you'll notice you will:

- Stand a little straighter—because you are speaking your authentic truth

- Find your tribe—because you'll attract more people like you

- Gain trust and respect—because you had the guts to step up in a bigger way

Your Terms of Use helps you to stand in your power and fully claim your work.

We're Tested Before We Expand

Have you ever noticed the timing of Copycats and Swipers striking your business? Often it's right before you're about to expand in your business. Tests can come just as you are getting ready to step up to a new level in your business income or visibility. I've seen it happen repeatedly, with myself and with other entrepreneurs.

I've noticed from working with hundreds of business owners that any leaks in our businesses that we might not have paid much attention to seem to show up right before we are raising our frequency to a higher level. Right before we're about to get bigger or receive more.

We see money leaks. Time leaks. Energy leaks. Boundary leaks. Relationship leaks. Lots of leaks. We see Swipers and Copycats prompting us to tighten our legal and energetic boundaries.

Here's what I've learned about energy: When we stretch and expand, sometimes issues or boundary leaks that need to be resolved emerge to make room for what's coming next.

You don't even have to believe in the energetic shift happening—it will happen anyway, whether you believe it will or not.

It's kind of like gravity—another principle involving an energetic pull. You don't have to believe in gravity, but it still happens anyway. Regardless of whether you choose to believe in the principle of gravity, gravity still exists. It doesn't matter whether you believe in it or not. Other energetic principles work the same way.

Leaks sideswipe you when you're busy looking the other way—like while you're planning your next big launch or product offer. It's like the Universe wants you to plug the leak because you're going to have so much more to lose as you get bigger and bigger, and you need to plug the leak now before you bare even more of your heart and soul to the world.

The Universe is testing you before you step up to the plate with the bases loaded. When you plug those leaks and bolster your boundaries, you send a message to the Universe that you're ready to receive more and that you're ready to hit a home run.

It's a horrible feeling when someone copies your course content or swipes parts of your opt-in gift, but sometimes it happens to get your attention so you can step in and shore up your boundaries.

Swipers and Copycats who try to snag your work show up to help you plug the leaks, close the gaps, recognize your value, and claim what's yours. We can't control when Copycats or Swipers strike, but we can be ready when they do. We can prepare by putting our Terms of Use in place. We can choose how we react when it happens. We can take legal action. We can trust that the truth always comes out in the end. We can trust that karma will catch up.

What we shouldn't do is hold back because we worry that someone will swipe our stuff.

Your Terms of Use give you a solid framework, thorough language, and a written document with clear terms to fall back on so you can enforce your policies. You can relax and let your voice be heard through your programs while feeling covered because you're using Terms of Use for your online sales.

Communication and Terms of Use Are
Aligned with the Throat Chakra

Sharing your message far and wide and expanding your communication through your online programs and products clearly aligns with the Throat Chakra.

The Throat Chakra is located, not surprisingly, at your throat. It incorporates your thyroid, parathyroid, jaw, neck, mouth, tongue, and larynx. Its name in Sanskrit, *Vishuddha,* means "pure place," which is a reminder to speak, listen and express yourself purely and with integrity.

The Throat Chakra is represented by the color light blue and is associated with speech, communication, self-expression, using your voice, sharing your dreams, listening, being heard, being understood, sharing your message and stating your truth.

Your Terms of Use protect what you create and disseminate, which reflect your truth and self-expression. When you put your Terms of Use in place, your communication boundary tightens and you honor your hard work.

When you create clearer lines in your communication, you find it gets easier to stand in your truth and express yourself more freely. When you express yourself more freely because you feel safely held by your legal protections, your energy expands.

From this expansive energetic state, your frequency rises. You feel more confident, more clear, and more courageous. You shift into a more ease-filled state because you aren't resisting your own expansion anymore, and you feel safe. You relax and allow, and you watch your programs thrive and your income increase.

When you start using Terms of Use for your online programs and products, your energy also shifts and you up your vibe. This added energetic benefit that comes after taking a legal step is yet another example of what I call "spiritual side effect of the law."

Next, we'll address what to do when you're scared to speak up or you feel blocked in your throat chakra. If you need an immediate boost, this Throat Chakra Mantra can help you set your intention for opening your throat energy and speaking more freely:

Throat Chakra Mantra

When you are seeking clearer communication in your life or business, you can set your intention using this Throat Chakra mantra:

"I am communicative. I am expressive. I am heard. I am understood."

Part of communicating clearly and expressing the truth of who you are is to decide and declare what you want, and then to claim and own what you believe.

It's not always easy to know what you want, who you are, and who you want to become. When you're setting your goals and holding the vision for your future business success, sometimes you can feel blocked. The future looks blurry. Images are vague. Ideas don't flow. You can't communicate what you want, and you have no idea how to put into words your deepest desires. This is normal.

When we're expanding as business owners, often we can feel alone. We don't know who is willing to support us on our journey. We aren't sure where we belong and who will be open to helping us uncover our hopes and dreams. We don't fit in with the nine-to-five crowd but we're not full-fledged business owners yet either. We're in between. We're between trapezes.

At all stages of entrepreneurship and business ownership, it's important to find a tribe. It's critical to find your peeps. It's essential to feel connected to a community and to feel supported and bolstered by others who speak your same language.

158

If you aren't sure where to find your tribe, or how to build your own, there's one place where everyone can start, and that's with a declaration about what we deeply and truly want... just for today.

Even if you can only see and communicate what you most want TODAY – in this moment –but not beyond, you can still declare your immediate desire, claim it and own it. Then you can allow yourself to attract and find people who meet you where you are to provide support, business relation-ships, and friendship.

Declare It, Claim It, Own It

Once you decide what you want for today—fully living from your heart, solely for you and not to please anyone else—the Universe conspires on your behalf to bring to you the tools, experiences, and opportunities to fully support you.

Once you clearly communicate what you want—and who you want to be—and you do it with certainty, circumstances magically rise to meet you. It's quite astounding when you realize that once you declare what you want, that which you most desire shows up for you more often with greater ease—whether it's more clients, more income, more visibility, more media attention, more friends, more free time, more freedom or more love.

But, to reap the benefits, you'll need to be aligned with it energetically.

The first step to doing that is to declare and claim EXACTLY what you want, in as much detail as possible, with the full belief that it has already happened.

Sounds crazy? Yeah, I know. It seems too easy and too hard at the same time to communicate what you want and who you want to be and then like magic people and events start showing up to support you. But that's how it works. Once you declare it, claim it, and own it, so it shall be.

Now, I need to warn you that it may not happen in the exact time frame that you wish or in the exact way that you envision, because there may be some lessons that you need to learn or some cobwebs to be cleared from your old wounds to be healed first, but if you are in true alignment with what you declare, claim, and own, and you have worked through any resistance to having what you want, inevitably it will happen.

---

3 Steps to Declare, Claim and Own Anything

How do you decide, declare, claim and own who you are and anything that you want?

So glad you asked.

1. **Declare it.** Get crystal clear about what you want your life and business to look like. Give your desires a voice, an image, a sound. Really get clear about your future vision. Where are you living? What are you doing? How do you spend your time? Journal about your ideal life, your ideal biz, your ideal clients. Grab some magazines and create an old-school vision board, or create a virtual one online. (If you need help getting clear, go back to Chapter 1 on Clarity and use the tools to reflect who you are and what you want.) Then write your vision down in your journal or on paper and read it aloud. To solidify your declaration as a done deal, you can even say at the end, "And so it is."

---

2. **Claim it.** Next, close your eyes and imagine what it would feel like to have it. Use all your senses to describe and feel what it would be like to have obtained it already. Claim it by fully sensing what you would be seeing, doing, and feeling if you'd already acquired it and claimed it as yours. How would you be feeling if your declaration were true today? Confident? Secure? Excited? Eager? Ready? How does it feel in your body? Butterflies in your stomach? Tense? Relaxed? Grounded? Strong? What does that feel like in your heart, soul and mind? Turn up the volume on the positive feelings and how good it feels to claim it.

3. **Own it.** Finally, imagine that that what you want is already here now and envision yourself communicating it to others. Time travel to the future and turn into those feelings as if they are happening right now and embody the sensory experience of what you are seeing, feeling, and doing. Own it viscerally as well as intellectually and energetically. It will come at a faster rate because you are already physiologically experiencing it as if it is real right now.

Amazing little trick, isn't it? Isn't it funny how to our minds, the future and the present are interchangeable? (We also explored this topic in Chapter 3 when we were finding our confidence through Resourcing and Pretending.)

Don't forget - people are waiting right now to hear from you right now. Your tribe. The people who resonate with you and your ideas—they want and expect you to be who you are. All of who you are.

But, your tribe doesn't know how to reach you if you haven't declared, claimed, or owned some part of your identity or your business yet.

I should know what that feels like. As I've been revealing in each one of these chapters, I am one of those people who has played small too. Even writing this book was scary for me and feels vulnerable to me. It's scary to claim my truth. It's scary to stand in my message. It's scary to say that I see legal protection as practical and also energetic in a way that is different than 99.9% of people in my profession. It took me a while to declare, claim, and own my expertise too. Don't beat yourself up about it. Just take baby steps and honor your vulnerability. We all feel vulnerable at times.

I've noticed that worrying about upsetting or triggering others is a big area of stress and distress for coaches and small business owners.

When you say or do anything outside of the box, the "crazies" can come out to attack, shame, or defame you.

Most people don't have the courage to speak their truth. Most people stay quiet and in the "box." Most are afraid to speak up, step forward or take a contrary position. It takes chutzpah to declare yourself an expert in your own knowledge or to share your core beliefs. It takes bravery to say, write, or teach concepts that change paradigms. It takes straight-up courage and a dose of confidence to show up fully.

But, if you feel called, you should step up, speak out, and contribute to the global conversation. The world needs to hear what you have to say and you will attract and find your tribe of supporters as you do so.

Show Up Fully Without Making Others Wrong

When you step up and share what you believe, you will inspire other people to be brave and that inspires still more people to do the same. It creates a ripple effect. Even if some think you are a maverick, there will be countless others who will thank the Universe that they discovered you because your message was exactly what they needed to hear.

If you speak from a heart-centered place with humility and grace, without making anyone else "wrong," your tribe will hear you and your truth will resonate.

Your tribe is seeking information that will give them solace, inspiration, hope or answers. They have been searching – sometimes for years or decades – to find someone like you who understands their journey and speaks directly to their deepest desires or painful wounds. They have been looking for someone to help them heal, thrive, accomplish or succeed. They haven't known it, but all along they've been looking for YOU.

Please don't deny them what they could learn from you because you are playing small and fear no one will want to hear what you want to say. It sounds cliché but even if one person's life is made better by your program, course, product, book, e-book or speech, then you've done your part in making the world a better place. Step around your Fear, and bring out your courage and clearly communicate what you feel called to say.

I can't tell you how many coaches, clients, and friends have said to me, "Lisa, I can't believe I've found you. No one talks about the law like you do from a spiritual side. You make understanding legal concepts so accessible and warm and understandable. I love your brand of Legal Love™. I never would have felt comfortable approaching other lawyers. You are such a bright light in the legal world. You inspire me to share my unique ideas, and I am so grateful to work with you and know you."

Wow. What a beautiful compliment. I am fortunate and grateful.

And as for the people who don't resonate with your message or beliefs, it's okay to send them love and light, and let them move forward in their own lives.

Give them the benefit of the doubt and trust that what they currently believe is right for them. You aren't trying to convince them otherwise.

You're simply trying to share your message with those who want to hear it.

I've lived long enough to know that there's room for more than one way to approach anything- and everything. As a lawyer, I can see both sides to any situation. That's exactly what they train us to do in law school. We learn how to see the pros and the cons, and not be the judge of either side. For certain, there are many ways to look at a situation or the world, and each person gets to decide what they believe is right for them.

In fact, there's really no need for judgment about whose approach is right and whose is wrong. I spent years of my past arguing and asserting my positions. I signed petitions and marched in marches, standing up for the rights of others. And while none of us should be oppressed in stating our views publicly or privately in a peaceful manner, as I've gotten older, I've learned that it's not healing for me to waste energy disagreeing or fighting with family or friends who don't share my beliefs. I've chosen to take the position that we can respectfully disagree, and love each other anyway. I believe that hate begets hate, and violence begets violence. I prefer to choose love and peace. I choose to "love the sinner and hate the sin."[12]

As I shared in the last chapter, I prefer to look at the world through the eyes of kindness, forgiveness, and goodness. (Remember, I'm not your typical lawyer.) I can be strong and ferocious if I need to be, but I prefer to leave contention and litigation to others.

I know that some people need to act like "warriors" and go all out to prove their point or passionately try make sure they have the last word. They use every argument they can find, even if it's excessive, and make assumptions based on their own fears. I was more that way when I was younger and approached everything as a threat, going in with guns-a'-blazing, but as I've gotten older and more secure and confident in myself, I know that throwing more hot air at something doesn't make it cool down.

Taking a position – any position – inevitably will attract your fans and trigger your foes. But, I believe it's better to stand for something, and serve those who resonate with your message than to hide in fear of those who don't. This is the true path of a "warrior"–speaking your mind and sharing your truth from a place of love and compassion, not attacking others or making them wrong.

While there may be some people who drift away from you for a reason, a season, or for life, on the flip side, you'll find a tribe of people who are even more engaged and loyal to you.

Losing Friends When You Speak Your Truth

As I've grown and deepened in my spiritual views about the law, sadly, a few friendships have waned a bit. Thankfully, many of my friends from law school are very open to my unique approach to the law, but other friends with more traditional religious backgrounds or world views are much less open, and it has created distance between us.

While my heart has broken watching a few strong friendships lessen in recent years, what I know for sure is that if others aren't open to concepts like listening to their intuition or living in alignment with what they know to be true, it's okay for me to step back, let them be, and to pause the friendship for now.

The majority of my friends, clients, and colleagues in my life "live in the light," as I like to say. They're open to alternative views of looking at the world, not afraid of their shadow selves, and not living in denial. They're open to self-introspection, self-awareness, and self-growth, and they don't live with their heads in the sand. They support me in becoming a better version of myself, and I do the same for them.

But not all are willing to view life through this lens, and that's okay. Neither of us is right or wrong; we just have differing outlooks. No way of looking at the world and no belief is absolute.[13] We each see the world through our own perspectives. We each view art, religion, politics, values, and life differently. We each vary in what we believe, know, and experience, and in United States we are free to think and believe what we wish.[14]

It's important to give each other basic love and respect, even when we differ in our political, religious, life, and world views. While I try to be respectful of others' feelings and beliefs, I also choose not to minimize what I believe, or deny what I know to be true.

It's hard for any of us to lose friends or slow friendships when we grow in a new direction or reveal deeply-held beliefs, but sometimes it's an unintended side effect of growth to let that which is no longer serving us fall away. Maybe as time evolves, my friends and I will reconnect, and I am very open to that.

I do know with certainty that the Universe always has my back, and that the friends I wish to have in my life hear my message, honor my philosophy, and support me completely, and I do the same for them.

Why We Can't Take Other People's Reactions Personally

We can't take other people's reactions personally, and here's why: It doesn't serve any of us if we squash our beliefs or diminish our values. What I try to remind myself is that other people's reactions to my thoughts or actions actually aren't even about me. They're about them.

Why is that?

Each person filters what others say and do through their own eyes and experiences.

Have you ever noticed that when you've shared a thought—like a strong political belief or controversial opinion—with someone and they have reacted with neutrality. They listened to you passionately express your thoughts, then they shrugged their shoulders and responded with, "Whatever you want to believe is fine. To each her own." They didn't get upset. They didn't engage in debate. They weren't triggered in any way to fight back or defend their own beliefs. My brother in law Bart is very much this way. He has strong beliefs, but he's very steady and even-keeled, and not much triggers him.

But then there are times you've shared that same belief with someone else and they abruptly snapped at you and raised their voice to say, "That's the stupidest thing I've ever heard! How can you even possibly believe that garbage? Are you really that idiotic?"

Yikes. The exact same statement. Two different responses.

You can feel attacked by the second response, but the truth of the matter is that their response wasn't about you or even about what you said.

Someone else's response has nothing to do with you.

Yes, that's right. Know that you are never, ever responsible for the thoughts, beliefs, or actions of someone else. No matter what anyone tries to tell you.

Others' choice of reaction (and, just to remind you, it's always a choice) about what they hear, filter, and interpret through their own belief systems does not involve you. Your comment may have unearthed their inner debate team, but you are not part of their internal filtering system, and therefore you are not responsible for their response. Ever.

Their response is never about you.

This realization that I am not responsible for anyone else's opinion of me was an enormous paradigm shift for me.

And as my friend and literary coach, Anjanette Fennell, always says, "You can't say the wrong thing to the right person, and you can't say the right thing to the wrong person."

You can't please everyone, and you won't. While you should use care and forethought with your words and actions, you are not responsible for others' reactions to what you do and say. Those reactions are their choice entirely.

They may argue that what you said upset them. But, what really happened is that you said something that threatened a belief (whether conscious or subconscious) or touched an open wound in them and they responded with strong emotion.

It's important to be sensitive to others' feelings and not deliberately say or do things that hurt others, of course. If you hurt someone, it's appropriate and loving to apologize that your words or actions hurt them. But you do not ever need to apologize for THEIR feelings, choices, actions, or responses, even when they think they have no control over them or try to blame you for the severity of their reaction.

Letting go of feeling responsible for other people's reactions is life-changing.

Other than parents caring for children or legal dependents, we are not responsible for other people and they are not responsible for us. We are not responsible FOR or TO each other. Shazam!

Key Takeaways from This Chapter

Once you decide to declare, claim and own your work and your message, give yourself permission to fully communicate your deepest message with truth, confidence, and grace.

Let yourself build and attract the business and life that you dream of based on your own unique brand and voice and be brave, step forward, and reach farther. Your future clients are dying to hear what you have to say.

As you do so, be sure to protect your passion, purpose, and products with the right legal steps like your Terms of Use so you can stop worrying that if someone steals your stuff you have no recourse. You also want to close any gaps, plug energy leaks, and tighten loose energetic boundaries so you'll be less likely to attract Copycats and Swipers in the first place.

Your fifth legal step is to use Terms of Use for Online Programs and Products.

Your fifth soul-centered principle is communication.

Your fifth chakra that is supported and aligned is your throat chakra.

Now It's Your Turn ...

Use this Legal Checklist and Business Self-Assessment to declare, claim and own your message and put your Terms of Use in place so you can stop Copycats and Swipers in their tracks and protect the online programs and products you've worked so hard to create.

Legal Checklist:

1. Do you have your Terms of Use in place on your sales page or shopping cart for all of your online programs, courses and products (everything except for one-on-one services)? (If so, you get a gold star!)

2. Are your Terms of Use long and robust enough to cover your policies about online commerce, refunds, communication, disclaimers, limitations of liability, and more?

3. Do you have a checkbox where purchasers can "check the box" and agree to your Terms of Use before they enter their credit card information? (If so, you get another gold star!)

4. Have you ever had to deal with a Copycat or Swiper? Did you know how to handle it? If not, do you know what to do now?

5. If you haven't gotten your Terms of Use in place yet, have you identified what's holding you back?

Business Self-Assessment:

1. How have you felt proud to speak your truth lately and share who you really are?

2. How can you take a baby step towards expressing yourself fully today?

3. Have you declared, claimed, and owned what you want?

4. Do you own your expert status? Can you consider yourself an "experiential expert"?

5. Have you lost friends because you have spoken your truth? How do you feel about that?

6. Do you tend to take other people's opinions of you personally? What can you do to shift that sense of responsibility?

7. Have you noticed boundary leaks showing up right before you're about to stretch and expand in your business or life?

Don't forget to grab your Legal Love™ Bonus Content!

Legal Love™ Bonus Content:

"Cease and Desist Letter" template to send to a Copycat or Swiper
who copies or uses your work without permission.
Free download at lisafraley.com/diyceaseanddesistletter
($197 value - Use code CEASE)

Chapter 6.

LLCs and S-Corps. Intuition. Third Eye Chakra.

For years, I didn't think that spirituality and logic could co-exist. **For the most part, I was raised to believe in what you can see, hear, smell, touch, and taste using our five senses.**

In law school, I was taught how to argue either side of any case (yes, even the most horrendous cases involving crimes like rape and murder) based on evidence that is apparent—and limited— to the five senses.

The law is historically based on logic and observable facts.

Evidence obtained through our five senses is viewed as mostly objective, though the degree can vary a bit from person to person as the strength of the senses is not the same in everyone. But in general, when it comes to law, reasonable observers can see, hear, smell, touch and taste the same things.

The legal system relies on judges and jurors to assess the facts of the court case and come to a rational, logical conclusion about what happened based on testimony that can be recognized by everyone involved. It's all about what you can argue and prove using the five senses.

Just the Facts, Ma'am

There is much less room for subjectivity in court[15]—that is, evidence which could be biased or offered merely as someone's opinion. For example, expert witnesses may offer their expert opinions,[16] but generally, other witnesses cannot. Witnesses are limited to offering testimony for which they have direct knowledge of the facts, unless their opinion is offered to clarify those facts.[17]

This is exactly what drives people nuts about the legal system, though. People get frustrated because the outcome of a case isn't always about what happened; it's about what you can PROVE happened. This is the only way to allow reasonable observers – like judges and juries – to declare an outcome and issue a ruling that is perceived as fair and objective.

If you are someone who uses more than just your five senses to interact with the world, or you make decisions based on information you have obtained through intuition or a higher power, limiting experiences to just the five senses can be bewildering, off-putting, and frustrating.

After all, intuition and spirituality are not concrete like logic and facts. They are not hard, physical evidence. Arguments based in natural law[18] and use of the "sixth sense" through higher power, intuition, spirituality, religion, divine guidance, or what I like to call "The Big 4 Clairs"[19] (clairvoyance, clairaudience, clairsentience, and claircognizance) do not have a place in the legal system.

Law and Spirituality are Intimately Interconnected

Law and spirituality are often viewed as opposite sides of the spectrum; yet, casting them as stark opposites isn't necessary. I believe they're intimately interconnected.

While intuitive hunches, divine guidance, and gut feelings can't be offered as evidence in court as there's no way to prove the objectivity of that type of evidence, they're highly important in how lawyers run their legal practices and lives—and how you as a business owner run your business and life as well.

I believe that lawyers have always done "spiritual" work, though I am guessing that many may not think in those terms, or would dare to describe themselves that way.

As I suggested in Chapter 4, lawyers often get a bad rap, which is unfortunate because so many of the lawyers I know are honest, caring, passionate and ethical. The bad apples out there seem to spoil the entire basket for the profession.

When I entered law school, I was a bright-eyed, bushy-tailed law student—and so were all of my friends. We entered the law school classroom wanting to learn how to stand up for others, fight for justice, seek legal reform, and give voice to people, causes, and principles. We wanted to support, protect, and defend others in a complicated and intimidating legal system. So many of us entered law school with big hearts and big goals.

What happens in law school, though, is that we're taught how to operate in the legal system so we could have careers in large law firms, small boutique practices, government branches, non-profit organizations and public interest agencies. This is a priority for law schools and one of the main roles of legal education, and I don't fault it. However, it often results in a shift from idealism to pragmatism as heart-centered dreamers learn how to become billable-hours-driven workers.

Ultimately, while many lawyers enjoy long, successful careers, a surprising number of big-hearted law students don't emotionally thrive in a system that is heavily adversarial and often viewed as soulless. Approximately 10,000 lawyers left the active practice of law altogether in 2014[20] and for many reasons, fewer students apply to law schools today than even five years ago.[21]

I know from personal experience that lawyers work long hours, regularly putting in 70-hour weeks and, though they're often paid handsomely, the tedious, detailed work of writing legal briefs or drafting corporate documents can take its toll on the mind, body, and spirit.

And if you find that you are someone like me with a strong empathic, feminine side in a structured, masculine law firm, you can see why I spent years stuffing down my emotions and intuition with bags of peanut M&Ms and boxes of marshmallow Peeps.

That Time I Ignored My Own Intuition

My out-of-control sugar addiction started long before law school, but revealed itself clearly when working at the law firm. I had no idea that I was different from anyone else and that my body processed sugar differently than others. I had no idea that I have always been an empath who sees, hears, feels, and knows things deeply and that I was using sugar to smoosh any emotion that didn't feel like happiness. I wasn't aware that I was trying to avoid feeling anger, frustration, fear, worry, anguish, anxiety, and distress—but I did notice that those emotions would just disappear once sugar entered my mouth.

The funny thing is that I had absolutely no idea that I was soothing my negative emotions with food until I was 42 years old. I had no clue.

I ended up leaving the practice of law altogether for a very long time. I thought that I didn't fit the mold and so I went on to serve the world in other values-aligned ways by working as a high-level development officer and non-profit fundraiser, raising over $7 million in major and planned gifts for charities and higher education, which felt good to my soul.

All along, I didn't realize that sugar was the culprit. I had thought that something was wrong with me as a person.

When I didn't realize that I was a sugar-sensitive, empathic woman, deep down, I feared that my talent, knowledge, experience, and disposition wasn't well-received by other lawyers, and part of me felt very out of place in a large law firm environment. Deep down, my intuition knew that despite my wonderful mentors who took great interest in the development of my career at the law firm, not being part of the law firm was the right decision, both for them and for me.

It was also a difficult decision for me to return to the law and to reinstate my law license over a decade later. I had thrown the whole legal baby out with the bathwater and didn't even know that I could focus on the parts of the legal practice that I loved—like helping clients go from stuck and scared of the law to feeling secure and confident so they could have the businesses and lives they wanted.

I'm glad that brought my heart back into the law and created a different kind of practice that can incorporate my formerly closeted beliefs about "the spiritual side to the law" and align legal steps with the chakras.

Had I known then what I know now, I would have avoided the discomfort, insecurity, and stress that I felt in the law firm that all parts of me weren't needed or valued there. I could have realized from day one that I could have my own practice to help entrepreneurs and small business owners. I didn't even know then it was an option.

Had I listened to my intuition sooner, I could have found deeper happiness faster.

Here's the thing though: I need to cut myself a little slack.

Back then I didn't know that my intuition was talking to me. I didn't know what my intuition and body were saying to me early in my legal career. I didn't know the Universe was nudging me in a different direction. I thought that my intuition was taking me off course. I didn't know it saw a clearer path than I did.

Just four months after I left the law firm and started as a non-profit major gifts fundraiser, I was recognized as one of Business First newspapers' "Forty Under 40" in Columbus, Ohio. I was only 29. There were so many other young business leaders in their 30s who had accomplished so much more who were overlooked that year who should have been acknowledged instead of me. I was astounded to be recognized, especially since I hadn't even nominated myself.

Looking back, I see that it was an external affirmation that shifting my professional focus from working in a large, private law firm to non-profit fundraising for charity was being honored. I was just the vehicle representing a rare move from a big firm to a non-profit organization. At the time, not many 29-year olds were making a professional shift in such a dramatic way. The public recognition was confirmation that I was on the right path, and that the firm and I had made the correct decision to part ways.

Never could I have predicted that when it comes to owning a business, I could have combined my love of the law, my interest in spirituality, and my desire to serve.

How I Brought Law and Chakras Together

It dawned on me one day while I was sitting in my office typing on my laptop that I could combine the legal and energetic sides of business to make the law more approachable, interesting, and holistic for entrepreneurs.

I had been looking at the vision board above my desk containing quotes like:

- "Whatever goal you give to your subconscious mind, it will work night and day to achieve." - Jack Canfield

- "You really don't have to try so hard. That's why there's magic and miracles. Remember?" – Mike Dooley

- "Create space for grace." – Nisha Moodley

I thought to myself: "Isn't it interesting that I'm a lawyer, and yet, all of the quotes on my vision board are about energy and spiritual principles? Clearly, I'm trained as a lawyer AND as a holistic health and life coach and both sides of me help my clients grow their businesses. Not only that, but understanding how the energy of the body works through the lens of the chakras makes so much sense to me."

Then it dawned on me that the seven most common steps that most entrepreneurs take in a particular order aligned almost magically with the seven chakras.

I realized that conscious entrepreneurs who care as much about doing soulfully aligned work as increasing their bank accounts would be open to me speaking about the law in a heart-centered way, and as needed, I could refer them to a few other lawyers I know who felt similarly.

I could diffuse fear for budding, boot-strapped entrepreneurs who wouldn't otherwise know where to turn for legal information or who didn't ever want to step foot in a law firm and make them more comfortable by speaking their–and my–soul-centered language.

I could bring together the woo side, the lawyer side and the coach side and I didn't have to choose among them. I didn't have to leave parts of me on the cutting room floor. By making the law feel easy and aligning legal steps with the chakras, I didn't have to keep these parts of me separated. Law and spirituality didn't have to be an "either/or" choice. I realized it could be an "and."

As you've seen throughout this book, the theme of "both/and" instead of "either/or" has become very meaningful for me. (This is precisely why I've had a lighted ampersand marquee in my office since 2013.)

By listening to my intuition and being open to divine inspiration, I could bring all of my interests together. The same is true for you.

You don't have to choose between parts of you in your own business. You can incorporate different aspects of your personality and align your work with your values in a way that keeps you feeling whole, rather than fragmented and scattered.

You don't have to struggle with what appear to be opposing interests or competing sides of your personality. You don't have to fight that you're intuitive and rational the same way that I no longer need to fight that I'm claircognizant AND a lawyer who also believes in logic and reason.

You can embrace the "and" and let all parts of you be fully expressed in your work.

Can you imagine what my life would have been like if I had listened to my intuition so many years ago and shifted gears to go out on my own then?

Thank goodness I finally learned how to tap into my intuition, or I never would have returned to law and helped so many passionate business owners support, protect and honor the businesses they have worked so hard to build.

If you aren't sure how to tap into your intuition, I'll share with you ways to get more internally connected, but first, let's talk about the legal step you need to know to protect the business YOU are working so hard to build. It's important to know the basics about how to protect your assets– both company and personal income and assets. You'll learn about the types of legal business entities that can hold and protect your business, and then we'll discuss the ways that you can unearth your intuition to better help you in every area of your life.

Your Legal Step: LLC or S-Corporation

One of the best ways to protect your business assets and income is to create a formal business entity—like an LLC or an S-Corporation (S-Corp).

Why should you create a corporate entity? There are multiple reasons.

6 Reasons to Go Pro with a Legal Business Entity

1. **To protect your assets.**

One of the best reasons to go pro is to protect your assets. If you're already financially successful or have a lot of personal assets, you may want to go pro now. Having a corporate structure in place will give you legal protection and keep your assets safe.

When you create a business entity like an LLC or S-Corp, you legally separate your personal assets from your business assets. This distinction is critical for keeping your finances and possessions unscathed. It's like putting a protective cloak around your business and belongings to keep them secure.

What the Heck are Assets?

Generally, there are two types of assets important to small business owners: personal assets and business assets. Your accountant can give you more thorough definitions as recognized by the Internal Revenue Service and state and local governments, because there are many different asset categories and they can be complicated.

Personal assets include property you own in the form of money or that can be converted to cash, like your house, car, savings accounts, investment accounts, insurance proceeds, vacation homes, income from other jobs, jewelry, and the inheritance from your late Aunt Edna.

Business assets include property or equipment purchased exclusively or primarily for business use. This could include your business real estate, cash in your business checking account, business savings account, accounts receivable (money owed to you for services rendered but not yet paid), office furniture, computer, cell phone, trademarks, copyrights, etc.

Note: These examples are intended to be general and indicative of assets commonly owned by small business owners. Please speak with your accountant to identify the assets of your business specifically.

2. **To limit your liability and exposure.**

Another reason to have a business entity is to limit your liability by separating yourself from your business. You want to keep them separated. Like separating paper from plastic. Like separating bickering children when you're at your wit's end. Like separating the men from the boys when you're looking for a promising date.

If a creditor comes after you for an unpaid business debt, provided you are following the proper procedures for your LLC or S-Corp, it means that they can only go after your business assets, and they can't collect unpaid debts by acquiring your personal assets. Likewise, if you are sued for a business issue, you aren't putting your personal assets, like your house or your car, at risk. You want to make sure you are limiting your liability so that people can't reach too deep into your pockets if they come after you or sue you.

3. **To save money on taxes and reap financial benefits.**

Having a corporate entity can give you serious financial benefits, especially over time. Right up front, you can deduct the formation of your LLC or S-Corp as a legitimate business expense and you can deduct the cost of any legal or financial help you receive from your lawyer or accountant as well.

Over time, your legal structure (especially an S-Corp) can give you more flexibility around income declaration when it comes to salary and distributions and often save you thousands in taxes. You can also reduce the risk of losing money in a lawsuit if you are ever sued.

4. To make your business "official" and raise your credibility.

When you create a business entity, it becomes official. You've filed the right paperwork at the state level to establish your LLC or corporation and you've instantly raised your credibility, whether you know it or not. When you "go pro," you're showing the world that you're taking your business more seriously—and as a result, everyone else takes it more seriously too.

No one can call your work "a kitchen table hobby" anymore. No one— not your spouse, your family, or your friends who may not totally get what you do—can diminish your work or devalue it by implying that because you're "doing it on the side" or you "just started" or you aren't in it to win it. When clients, friends, other business owners, and potential clients see the "LLC" or "Inc." or "Corp." after your business name, they know you're raising your professionalism big-time and your business is the real deal.

5. To give you peace of mind as you play bigger.

When you play bigger, you may feel cautious. Your business is its own "thing" with its own personality, energy, containers, and goals. This is exciting because it holds big possibilities for what you want for your future, but sometimes you can worry that it will grow faster than a rate you can comfortably handle. You might worry that it will suck your time or your energy or you will be bombarded with new clients or a bazillion e-mails and you'll drown in business tasks.

Your business can grow and expand at whatever rate you allow, and it can bring you all that you want as you grow with it. But having an entity that is and feels separate from you can give you peace of mind that it is not you. Your business is held and protected in a compassionate container that is separate from you.

6. **To energetically expand as you take small steps (and big leaps!) forward.**

Another reason to create a business entity is to open yourself to growth by creating your formal business entity. Establishing your business is a milestone to be celebrated. It has huge emotional and spiritual effects on you as a business owner. Forming a corporate entity causes something to energetically shift within you. Upleveling happens every single time that an entrepreneur or biz owner receives confirmation in the mail that their entity has been formed. My clients tell me over again that they feel more confident, secure, stable, and proud.

Not only do you protect your assets and limit your liability, but your energy shifts and you lean into expansiveness because you've created a legal container to protect and hold your potential business growth and all of the future income that can come your way. Your business entity holds the expansion of your business, dreams, income and lifestyle. It creates a loving legal container to support your business as you take small steps and big leaps toward your future. You start to attract even bigger opportunities that you couldn't have dreamed of.

So now that you know why a corporate entity can benefit you, what are your options?

Structuring your business properly and protecting your assets is important. For most solo business owners, there are three commonly used options for legally structuring a business: Sole Proprietorship, Limited Liability Company (LLC), Corporation (most often as an S-Corporation).

> ## A Little Disclaimer About Big Business Entities
>
> Please note that the legal information in this chapter is designed to give you a place to start, and like everything else in this book, is intended to be educational and informational to point you in the right direction. It isn't to be relied upon as legal advice for your specific business.
>
> When it comes to creating a business entity, there are many factors that you need to take into consideration. Be sure to work with your own attorney and accountant to determine which structure is right for you based on your situation, goals, finances, expertise and business type.
>
> You want an accountant and a lawyer who "get what you do" as a coach or entrepreneur and who are willing to grow with you and enlighten you about the legal structure that is best suited for your business and who can inform you about your local, state, and federal laws.

The 3 Most Common Business Structures for Solo Business Owners

1. Sole Proprietorship—The Simplest Way to Get Started

When you are starting out as a solo biz owner, as you know from Chapter 3, you are considered a Sole Proprietor, which is the simplest form of a business structure. (Don't forget to register your business locally with the city, county and even the state as explained in Chapter 3.)

Hanging out your shingle as a Sole Proprietor is the easiest way to get rolling, but it also has the most risk. When the time is right, you may want to form a corporate entity like an LLC or S-Corporation for more legal protection for any of the six reasons outlined above.

When you're ready to go pro, the first step that most entrepreneurs and small business owners take when transitioning from a Sole Proprietor is to form a Limited Liability Company.

2.   Limited Liability Company—The Easy Business Structure

A Limited Liability Company (LLC) is a company that you form at the state level. It's an actual company with its own identity, and it's legally separate from you. It's a basic legal entity designed to give you protection by limiting your liability as a business owner by separating your business assets from your personal assets to stop the reach of creditors.

The LLC is a simple entity – it does not have a board of directors or officers like a corporation. You as the owner are called a "member." It's an uncomplicated organization that requires little paperwork or corporate maintenance, other than an annual filing and fee required by most states. Once it's set up properly, it's designed to give its owners flexibility with few corporate responsibilities. That's why small business owners love it.

Not to get too legal-speak, but an LLC is referred to as a "pass-through entity." What that means is that the company itself is "disregarded" by the IRS and not taxed at the business entity level (unlike a corporation which IS taxed at the corporate level). The income that you receive from your LLC is "passed through" the LLC and declared as your personal income on your individual tax return.

What this means for you is that you pay taxes on your revenue as the business owner, but the LLC corporate structure itself does not pay taxes as a business entity. You've heard people talk about how corporations pay "corporate taxes", right? Well, unlike corporations, the LLC itself doesn't pay taxes; only YOU do as the member. You report your income from the LLC on your individual tax return. This simplifies things for you, but gives you the asset protection of a legal entity. It's ideal for many budding business owners.

As a sole business owner, many choose to have their income taxed as an individual (income is reported on your individual tax return just like as a Sole Proprietor) but you are also given the option of being taxed as a corporation (income is reported on quarterly corporate tax returns). For various reasons, you may "elect" to have your LLC to be taxed as an S-corporation.[22] This is a more complicated option, but it can be financially beneficial in the long run. There are, of course, pros and cons for both choices. Your accountant can help you determine which is the best option for you.

When taxed as an individual, the LLC is an easy corporate entity to create and maintain, and it gives you asset protection and limited liability that you don't get as a Sole Proprietor.

Even with the simplicity of an LLC, however, there are requirements you must follow, such as:

- **You must make it obvious that you have an LLC** which means including the name of your LLC on your website, marketing materials, business cards, invoices and more. This is important for protecting your LLC status and identity should you be challenged in a lawsuit. Always include "LLC" after the name of your company – on everything.

- **You can't "comingle" your funds.** You need to have bank accounts and accounting records for your LLC that are different from your personal accounts. You can't mix or "comingle" your funds. Set up a bank account in the name of your LLC and make all income deposits and expense withdrawals through that account. Do not use your business account to directly withdraw money for personal shopping or living expenses. Keep your income and expenses for your business separate from your personal life.

- **You'll need at least one business bank account set up for your LLC** for your business transactions, including depositing your business income and withdrawing money for your business

185

expenses. When you want to pay yourself, transfer money to your personal bank account from your business account. Pay all of your personal expenses from your personal banking account, not your business account. Use your personal banking account for personal expenses.

The Pros and Cons of an LLC

The benefits of an LLC are:

- Good asset protection—it separates your personal and business assets

- Limits your personal liability (your buns are covered!)

- Easy structure to create

- Requires little ongoing maintenance except for filing an annual report, fee, and perhaps local franchise tax registration documents based on your location

- Provides tax and estate planning options

- Flexible to operate

- Fairly inexpensive after initial investment of LLC creation

- Does not require the filing of a separate tax return for the LLC itself

- Costs of forming and maintaining an LLC are legitimate business expenses

- The downsides of an LLC are:

- Not a lot of tax flexibility

- If elect to be taxed as an individual, requires payment of self-employment tax (basically Social Security and Medicare taxes)

- If elect to be taxed as a corporation, requires greater expense, attention and reporting

Note: This is not an exhaustive list. These are just highlights some of the key pros and cons.

When you operate an LLC as a solo business owner, you can expect to spend a few thousand dollars to have a lawyer create it for you. This is normal. It's worth having an attorney set it up correctly from the start so you know it has been done properly and you don't have to worry.

An attorney can also help you determine in which state to create it, whether you want to have a registered agent in place, create your LLC agreement, obtain your federal tax ID number, and talk through with you exactly what each LLC document is, when you'll need it, and what you need to do on an ongoing basis to maintain your LLC.

Be sure to work with an attorney who takes the time to make you feel comfortable, confident, and empowered, and who tells you how to open your corporate bank account, where to include "LLC" in your marketing materials, how to properly keep your business records, and how to renew your LLC annually, which is required in most states.

Can I Create an LLC Without Hiring a Lawyer?

Can you create your LLC without hiring a lawyer? Yes, you can. You can use an online legal service or create it through your state directly, but it's not recommended unless you've had an LLC previously or you know how to set them up properly.

You want to make sure that you are selecting the right business entity for you, filing the paperwork correctly, completing all of the documents you need, and aware of your state requirements for annual renewal and reporting. Some states require additional tax forms or business licenses needed at the state or local level that may not be obvious to you or instructed by an online legal service.

Doing legal work on your own is like anything else, right? If you know what you're doing and you're confident you are doing it correctly, you can save money and do it yourself. However, having a professional do it for you is usually a wise move. There's nothing more frustrating than paying money, trying it on your own, and doing it wrong which can expose you to risk. Knowing your LLC is set up properly and receiving personalized attention are worth every penny.

3. Corporation—The Most Complex Business Entity

The third option is to create a Corporation. I know that having a Corporation can sound daunting, particularly if you're a one-woman or one-man show, but corporations are a great option if you are farther along with your business or in certain instances.

There are two main types of for-profit corporations: S-Corporations, which we'll address in this chapter, and C-Corporations[23].

While some solo business owners create C-Corporations, most opt to establish S-Corporations or elect to have their LLC taxed as an S-Corp, so this conversation is limited to the pros and cons of creating S-Corps.

In general, a corporation is a business entity that has its own legal identity, rights, powers, and duties. Its owners are called shareholders. It's governed by a board of directors and its management team members are called officers. When you think of a large corporation, you may think of companies like Starbucks® or Apple® or Nike®. These are examples of C-Corporations.

However, corporations may also have just one owner. Many of my clients are surprised to learn that you can have a corporation with just one shareholder, one director, and one officer (serving as both the president and the secretary)—and that's YOU! When you're the only one running the show, you may want to create an S-Corporation (or S-Corp, for short).

What's an S-Corp, Exactly?

An S-Corporation is a corporation which has elected to be taxed differently than a regular C-Corporation. The "S" refers to Subchapter S of the Internal Revenue Code, but I always say the easiest way to keep them straight is to remember that the "S" correlates to a "small" corporation. (That's not a legal definition—that's just my handy way to remember which is which.)

If you want to create an S-Corp, you first create a corporation at the state level and then you file paperwork with the IRS to be granted Subchapter S status at the federal level. (In some states, you also need to file paperwork at the state level too.) If a corporation elects Subchapter S status, it means that the corporation receives the benefits of being a corporation, but gets the extra bonus of being taxed as a "pass-through entity" (just like an LLC), so the corporate entity itself doesn't have to pay taxes.

The corporation still must file tax returns, but there's no income tax imposed at the corporate level. This means that it has the potential to save you a significant money over time. No joke. That's one of the main reasons a lot of business owners elect S-Corp status.

S-Corporations are much more demanding than LLCs, however, both in time and in dollars. You'll pay taxes on the corporate tax schedule (generally four times per year), determine salary and payroll taxes, and have increased bookkeeping tasks which means you'll want your accountant to play an active role. Because of the additional work required for more frequent tax preparation and corporate tax filings, your accounting costs can increase considerably.

Also, there are more corporate requirements for S-Corps than for LLCs, including holding annual meetings of shareholders and directors (even if it's just you!), recording corporate minutes, and operating more formally as a business entity.

Nevertheless, having an S-Corp is a good option once your business is over six figures in income because often you can save money in taxes, especially over time (but check with your accountant to discuss your own circumstances.)

There are 2 ways to become an S-Corp:

1. **By electing S-Corp Status as an existing LLC.** If you already have an LLC, you simply file the S-Corp election form with the IRS within 90 days after formation of the LLC and you receive S-Corp status. (There are exceptions to the 90-day rule, but speak to an attorney or accountant for assistance.) Electing S-Corp status is an easy way to receive the benefits of an S-Corp without having to dissolve your LLC and start over with an S-Corp which can involve time, money and hassle.

2. **By creating a new S-Corp.** If you don't have any corporate entity in place, you may choose to create a new S-Corp by creating a corporation at the state level and then filing the S-Corp election form with the IRS. If your income is quite substantial, it may make sense for you to go from being a Sole Proprietor directly to forming an S-Corp.

One of the drawbacks to forming an S-Corp is that all shareholders must be U.S. citizens. That means that if you want to form a company with your bestie who lives in London and she's a U.K. citizen, you won't be able to form an S-Corp. (You'll be able to form a C-Corporation, however.)

The Pros and Cons of an S-Corp

The benefits of creating an S-Corp are:

- Much more tax flexibility around declaring your income as salary or as distributions—which have different tax implications (you still must pay taxes on all of your income, of course!)

- Possible significant tax savings—this is the primary reason for forming an S-Corp, and it can far outweigh the downsides

- Easy transfer of shares if you wish to sell your interest in your S-Corp

- Costs to create and maintain the S-Corp and paying a lawyer and an accountant to help you are legitimate business expenses

The downsides of creating an S-Corp are:

- More complicated to create

- Must establish salaries, payroll deductions, and distributions and pay payroll tax (FITA, FUCA, and income tax withholding)

- More complicated to maintain on an annual basis

- Must follow proper corporate record-keeping, hold annual meetings, and record minutes

- Foreign corporations formed outside the US may not elect to be S-Corps

---

- Cannot have more than 100 shareholders (which isn't a problem for solopreneurs!)

- All shareholders of S-Corps must be US citizens

- Must use the cash method of accounting (which means you record income from sales when the payment is received and expenses when they are paid)

- Can have only one class of stock (which isn't an issue for solopreneurs but can be limiting if you want to have investors who are paid different distribution amounts than shareholders)

- Some states require a separate form to be filed at the state level as they don't honor the federal S-Corp election form

- There are timeframes around when the S-Corp election form should be filed or there can be additional ramifications

- If you ever want to convert your S-Corp to a different type of business entity, it may involve greater costs based on built-up appreciation in the value of the business.

- Sometimes triggers greater IRS scrutiny to make sure that salary and distributions are accurate and reasonable.

WHEW! See what I mean when I said that S-Corps are more complex?

Note: This is not an exhaustive list. These are just highlights of the key pros and cons.

Thank You, IRS!

Thank your lucky stars – and then thank the IRS! (Seriously. I'm not kidding.) The IRS gives small business owners a tremendous gift wrapped up in a big red bow. They allow you to start out as a Sole Proprietor, then create an LLC as you expand, and then elect S-Corp status without having to shut down and dissolve your LLC and form a new S-Corp.

TA DA! This is a huge gift to you because to shut down and dissolve a business entity requires time, money, and the headache of having to change information on bank accounts, invoices, credit cards, tax forms, business cards, and lots of other paperwork.

Instead, you can keep your LLC and get the financial benefits and tax flexibility of an S-Corp without having to disrupt your business structure and updating umpteen documents. So the next time that you want to complain about the IRS, remember that the ability to elect S-Corp tax status is a gigantic gift from the IRS to entrepreneurs and small businesses, and then drop to your knees and thank the government for this immense gift. Trust me.

Now that we've addressed the three main types of business entities for small biz owners, when is the right time to go pro?

When's the Right Time to "Go Pro" with an LLC or S-Corp?

Like with many things legal, a simple question does not always result in a simple answer. The simple answer is that it depends on your individual situation. (You knew I was going to say that, right?) But there are some general rules of thumb that can help.

If you have substantial personal assets or business assets, you'll likely want to create an LLC or S-Corp sooner rather than later.

A general ball park figure for forming an LLC is once you have approximately $50,000 in gross revenue.

A growing business with revenue of $50,000 is nothing to sneeze at. You now have substantial income that you don't want to lose, it's a good time to think about going pro, but you'll want your accountant to assess your entire financial picture before deciding if an LLC is right for you.

Once your income surpasses $100,000, it's a good time to form an S-Corp.

Once you reach six figures, it's a good time to form an S-Corp from scratch, or elect to having your LLC taxed as an S-Corp. Again, that's a ball park figure, so talk with your accountant to be sure that the legal costs of creating the S-Corp and accounting costs to file tax returns are worthwhile for your specific situation.

If you have significant personal assets, regardless of whether you have a start-up business or you are already making multi-six figures, talk with your attorney and accountant about protecting yourself now rather than leaving all of your assets naked and exposed.

If you don't have personal assets or business assets yet, you may want to wait. If you're investing your assets in your business by creating your website, enrolling in training programs, hiring coaches and attending conferences, you may want to put some of the other legal steps in this book in place first to protect your work and your income (like your Client Agreement for your one-on-one services and your Terms of Use for your group programs and online courses) BEFORE you protect your assets since your assets are fewer.

Many lawyers will encourage you to create an LLC right out of the gate when you form a business. I don't always agree with that approach because an LLC can only help you from a liability standpoint AFTER you get sued. That's right. It only helps you AFTER someone comes after you and tries to get their paws on your assets.

You are often wise to devote your limited funds to contracts, documents and disclaimers that can help you build your legal toolbox and stop people from coming after you in the first place.

Remember that signed legal documents can be used to remind clients of what they agreed to at the outset which can often quell a lawsuit. Written contracts that include clauses to provide for alternative dispute resolution and limited remedies can deescalate emotional situations before they explode. Because I take a holistic and preventative approach to everything in life and business, I'd prefer you put your limited resources into stopping problems before they start.

You should know that anyone can file a lawsuit against anyone at any time. People can file a claim for just about anything. But that doesn't mean that their lawsuit has merit. Your written and signed legal documents can help diffuse a firestorm and keep it from turning into a lawsuit.

The way I see it as a Holistic Lawyer®, your legal documents are like green smoothies for your business.

Your legal documents keep your business strong and your immunity high. When it comes to liability, your LLC and S-Corp can keep you from having to visit the doctor when you get run down and exhausted and you catch the flu bug. It's better to not get sick in the first place by fueling your business with vitamins, minerals, and other nutrients it needs to stay strong and healthy.

So, if you have few personal or business assets right now, I encourage you to put your limited dollars and time into protecting the money that clients are paying you so you can accumulate it, gain more assets AND then create your LLC or S-Corp. Make sense?

In short, if you have a lot of personal or business assets already, think about creating your legal business entity now. If you don't have a lot of assets, hold off and focus on protecting your income and work first.

Selecting the right business entity for you is a big decision. Please don't feel overwhelmed by deciding which corporate structure is the best option for your business and let it keep you stuck and small. Use the chart below as a quick reference and talk with an attorney and accountant to make the right decision for you.

(Not sure what to ask when interviewing an attorney, grab "10 Questions to Ask When Hiring an Attorney" in the Legal Love™ Bonus Content at the end of the chapter – and remember you can grab "10

Questions to Ask When Hiring an Accountant" in the Bonus Content at the end of Chapter 3.)

Which Type of Business Entity Is Right for You?

As I've mentioned repeatedly, be sure to talk with an attorney and accountant to determine which business structure is right for you. But, here's a handy-dandy summary at quick glance:

A Sole Proprietorship might be right for you if you're:

- A brand new business owner

- Only wanting a side business or a part-time gig

- Not making much income yet

An LLC might be right for you if you're:

- A fairly new business owner

- Not possessing a lot of business assets

- All about simplicity

- Not able to easily predict your monthly income because it fluctuates too much

- Making about $50,000 in annual gross income (this is a good ball park figure but talk with your accountant) OR you have a lot of personal assets

An S-Corp might be right for you if you're:

- An established entrepreneur

- Bringing in consistently high income

- Comfortable with complexity

- Recording predictable and stable income and expenses

- Happy to pay a team for legal and accounting work

- Making over $100,000 in annual gross income (this is a good ball park figure but talk with your accountant) OR you have a lot of personal or business assets

Avoiding the legal parts of your business obstructs your growth.

That's why legal planning and preparation—like understanding the basics about corporate entities—is so important and knowing about your options is critical.

Putting in the time effort to set your business up correctly keeps you from later having to worry about it crumbling down or spending half of your time doing damage control. Legal Pickles™ and lawsuits can cost you dearly—not just in terms of dollars and time, but in emotional toll, energy drain and distractions from what's important, which is building your business and serving your clients.

Set yourself up for success and abundance right from the start. Trust your intuition when you have a sense that it's time to "go pro" and elevate yourself to the next level of professionalism and energy frequency by creating your business entity. Then trust your lawyer and your accountant to have your back.

Intuition and Corporate Entities Align
with the Third Eye Chakra

I like to say that "you always know when it's time to go pro."

I love that the third eye chakra is called *Ajna* in Sanskrit which means "beyond wisdom." The third eye chakra is located right in the center of your forehead between your eyebrows and is represented by the color indigo. It's

197

associated with principles like intuition, inner knowing, internal guidance, insight, vision, focus, wisdom and consciousness.

In my view, corporate entities are aligned with the third eye chakra because forming an LLC or S-Corp taps into your inner insight. Many of my clients have told me they "just knew" it was time to take their business up a notch and to make their operation more "official." They trusted their intuition that it was time to talk with an attorney and accountant about going pro with a corporate entity.

In addition to seeking advice and assistance from experts, we can listen to our intuition when it comes to business and follow the nudges we get to expand our expertise, launch a new program, create a new product or develop a new service.

No one else has your vision for yourself and your future. Remember, no one else has the same wisdom or insight as you or a combination of what you offer when you bring your gifts together. Not another single soul has:

- Your vast professional and life experiences.

- Your unique combination of training, education, knowledge, and expertise.

- Your personality, heart, presence, and grace.

- Your inner knowing, sixth sense or connection to your inner wisdom

Listening to your intuition and following your inner whispers allow you to dare to dream big for your business, take a stand for your values, follow your desires, and satisfy the deepest parts of you.

To set your intention for going pro, you can use this Third Eye Chakra Mantra to remind you to tap into your intuition, listen to those gentle nudges, and raise your professionalism when the time feels right.

> ### Third Eye Chakra Mantra
>
> When you want to tap into your intuition for answers
> in life or business,
> you can set your intention using this Third Eye Chakra mantra:
>
> *I am intuitive. I am guided. I am focused. I am insightful.*

So many entrepreneurs and small business owners find themselves in the energetic frequency of fear, distrust, worry, nervousness, anxiety and distress, and not listening to their own intuition—just like I did when I worked at the law firm.

They don't know how to combine the practicalities of running a business with their intuition's desire to give, serve, teach, and support their clients. It can feel like such an uncomfortable juxtaposition of service and profit—because to be able to serve, you need money to live.

The problem is that we can keep searching and searching externally for answers from coaches and courses and colleagues, without taking any time to look inward for spiritual nudges and answers, or to listen and watch for signs, messages, or guidance.

Sometimes we just need to take a deep breath, settle in, close our eyes and ask ourselves: "What do I really need right now to grow my business? What step feels most aligned for me to take? What do I really want in this moment?"

We can tune into our voice of intuition to find out what is right for us at any given time.

Our Intuition Is Always Talking to Us

Our intuition is always talking to us. It's whispering, guiding, nudging, and communicating with us.

Our intuition and gut knows when it feels right to take the next steps in your business. Take note. If you're waffling about something in your life or work, your inner wisdom already knows the answer.

With so much external noise in our daily lives, from whirring computers to incessant social media posts to constantly ringing cell phones, it can be hard to sift through the interference.

Often we need to just get quiet and create the space to listen to our own voices and tap into what we already know to be true.

If you struggle to tap into your intuition or you aren't sure if you are really accessing it, you are not alone. Many people aren't sure what their intuition wants them to know—or how to even find out.

And before I dive into telling you how you can access your intuition, I want to acknowledge you if you might be feeling any fears, discomfort, or trepidation right now. There can be times when we all might feel a bit afraid to tune in to get answers.

If we've been struggling with something for a while, we may fear that if a deep truth or answer comes to light, it might mean that we will feel prompted to do something uncomfortable. Things that might be scary. Things that might require change. Things that might hurt other people.

---

10 Things We Might Not Want to Do After Tapping into Our Intuition

Sometimes, we're afraid to listen to that little voice inside because we are afraid that we'll feel called to take a step that feels terrifying or uncomfortable. That's why it's sometimes easier to ignore our intuition. It might want us to:

1. Step outside of our comfort zone.

2. Distance ourselves from someone we love.

---

3. Change the way we do things—eat, sleep, work, play, exercise, relax, or live.

4. Give up something that feels familiar but that isn't serving our highest good.

5. Take an action towards something that we want, even though it feels terrifying.

6. Shift our "story" about what's happened in the past that keeps us safe and small.

7. Hold a new vision about our future success because we might be bowled over by it.

8. Own our uniqueness because it taps into our fear of not belonging.

9. Take a stand for what we know to be true, even if that creates waves.

10. Honor ourselves over everyone else, fearing we'll be told we're selfish or self-centered.

It takes bravery to tap into our intuition and be willing to hear what it says.

It takes someone who values wanting to know the truth of what their soul desires. It takes someone who wants to align their life, words, actions and beliefs with what feels right for them in their soul. It takes someone with courage.

Just because your intuition tells you something that you know is a soul-level truth may not mean you're ready to act on it just yet. You may need some time to process what you uncover, to understand how it fits into your present circumstances, to create a plan to make shifts. You may need time to digest your discoveries. And that's okay.

Listening to your intuition takes someone who also knows that you have the choice whether to act on what you hear ... or not.

Every day is about making choices. Choices about how to work and live however you wish, in whatever way serves you best.

You always have a choice ... and knowing that you have a choice is empowering.

Even When Your Hands Are Tied, You Still Have a Choice

You know when people tell you a story about something that happened, when they felt backed into a corner and they explain the outcome by saying, "I had no choice but to do what I did. I felt like they had a gun to my head."

Well, as I have learned from my husband, who is a decorated military veteran, even if someone has a gun to your head, you still have a choice.

Let me say that again. Even if there's a gun to your head, you still have a choice.

Let that one land for a moment.

In fact, what I've learned from my husband is that you always have many choices. Even if someone has a gun to your head, you have lots of options: You can choose whether to use your hand to knock the gun out of the way. You can choose to duck. You can extend your leg and kick the back of the perpetrator's knee so he or she falls to the floor. You can ask for the gun to be laid on the ground. You can signal for help. You can choose to create a distraction and try to escape. These are just a few of the possibilities.

There are always many, many options—even in situations when it would seem as if you don't have options, like when there's a gun pointed to your head. You may not LIKE the options in front of you, but remembering that you almost always have choice in most situations is deeply empowering.

On an every-day basis, you can choose what to think. You can choose your actions and choose your reactions. Even when your reactions feel automatic, they're likely just habits which can be changed. You can choose whether to express calm emotions or get visibly upset. You can choose whether to sit still and ponder about something, or decide to get up and go for a walk. Having a choice – and remembering that you have a choice - is powerful.

You get to decide.

If your intuition is leading you to sign up for a program—or NOT to sign up for a program—or to sell your business and travel around the world, or to hunker down and save money and travel around next year, you have the privilege of deciding what you do with the information that your intuition reveals to you.

You are still in control of your circumstances.

Knowing that you get to decide whether to act on your intuition or not can alleviate some of the fear or hesitation you might have when tuning inward to discover your inner wisdom. Even when you become aware of your intuitive guidance and hunches, you still get to decide what you do with them. Let that give you comfort as you open into tapping into your inner wisdom on a more frequent basis.

How to Access Your Intuition

Have you ever had a moment when unexpectedly out of the blue you just "know" that something is true? Like when something just "pops" into your head and without knowing any facts or circumstances. This sense of "just knowing" is like claircognizance when you gain information about a person, object, place, or event through intrinsic knowledge that has no external factual validation.

Sometimes our inner knowing reveals our true desires in what seems like odd puzzle pieces—things like a few words from a song, an image of the ocean or a bird, a series of numbers, the scent of an essential oil, or other seemingly random bits of information.

You can receive energetic messages from your inner wisdom when you least expect it. Sometimes your intuition gives you spontaneous messages. Other times, you can access your intuition deliberately through meditation, prayer, or silent walks in nature.

When you pay attention and tune into any little sign you receive, your inner knowing can point you in the right direction in life, business, relationships, self-care, family, health, wellness, sensuality, and every area of your life.

I know for me that I can get "intuitive hits" in mid-afternoon when I pop from my home office into the kitchen for a cup of green tea and an apple. Or, when I'm out running on the trails behind my house, an intuitive flash will land and I'll know exactly what it means. Other times, I may see certain birds, hear snippets from songs or TV ads, or see repeating numbers and those symbols, words, images, and feelings mean something to me beyond their face value. Their message may be revealed to me in the most divine of timing, either right then or later on. I now know that I want to be open to the information I receive from all sources, not just to information derived through my five senses.

When you listen to your intuition, you receive answers from yourself and the Universe about how to support, protect and grow your business and improve your life.

Intuition grows stronger the more you use it, so the more you practice tuning in, the faster you will access it.

Try This If You're Having Trouble Tapping In   ·

If you're having a tough time hearing what your intuition is trying to tell you, try this:

1. Pause what you are doing, silence your phone, get quiet, and remove distractions.

2. Set your intention by saying to yourself (silently or aloud): "It's my intention to access my intuition right now." Keep an open heart and mind. Be curious as to what your inner knowing wants to share.

3. Take three deep breaths.

4. Tune into your body and sense where you are carrying any muscle tension. Take a deep breath and visualize each area of tension relaxing, one area at a time.

5. Ask yourself a question to which you are seeking an answer (silently or aloud).

6. If you hear your inner critic jabbering in your ear, saying seemingly logical things like "Why are you wasting your time doing this silly exercise? This will never work. You have so much to do. Stop this right now and get back to work", imagine turning the volume down in your head so you can barely hear that voice anymore. At the same time, acknowledge the voice by saying (silently or aloud), "Thank you. I hear you and I acknowledge what you're saying, but I am going to continue with asking my intuition to come forward." That usually quiets the voice, at least for a time.

7. Take another deep breath, be open and see what other thoughts come up for you.

8. Notice where your body won't let go of tension, particularly if you ask a "yes" or "no" question. Tension can be a form of resistance where your body tries to brace you for the impact of the answer. (Our bodies are smart!) Lean into the tension, and while this may sound crazy, ask the tension what it is trying to protect you from hearing. You might be surprised as to what your inner knowing tells you. Be gentle with yourself and be open to the answer.

9. Once you've concluded, grab a journal or computer and jot down any words, images, smells, sounds, feelings, or certainties that you saw, heard, smelled, felt or "just knew." It might not make sense to you in the moment how they're linked to the question you posed, but it might dawn on you later how they are connected, and then you'll have your answer.

Key Takeaways from This Chapter

Let your LLC or S-Corp support you and protect your business in a practical way, and let your intuition, wisdom and vision take you exactly where you want to go as you move forward in your business.

Your sixth legal step is to go pro with an LLC or S-Corp.

Your sixth soul-centered principle is intuition.

Your sixth chakra that is supported and aligned is your third eye chakra.

Now It's Your Turn …

Use this Legal Checklist and Business Self-Assessment to tap into your intuition, follow your own knowledge and wisdom and go pro with an LLC or S-Corp when the time is right for you.

Legal Checklist:

1. Do you already have your LLC or S-Corp for your business? (If so, you get a gold star!)

2. Do you have significant personal assets or business assets to protect?

3. Have you felt an inner nudge to "go pro" to kick your professionalism up a level?

4. Do you have a lawyer you can turn to for assistance with forming your corporate entity? (If so, you get another gold star!)

5. Do you already have an accountant on your team? (You get another gold star!)

6. If you haven't gotten your LLC or S-Corp in place yet, have you identified what's holding you back?

Business Self-Assessment:

1. Do you believe there's room for both logic and intuition when it comes to life and business?

2. Do you notice when you hear inner whispers or gentle nudges from your intuition?

3. How do you receive information using your "sixth sense"—through images, sounds, smells, taste, touch, feelings, or knowing?

4. Do the nudges you receive scare you so that you shove them down with sugar, shopping, work or some other distraction?

5. Take a moment to think back to when you "just knew" the truth about something and you didn't follow your gut. Thinking back now, would you have made a different choice? Would you make the same choice today?

Don't forget to grab your Legal Love™ Bonus Content!

Legal Love™ Bonus Content:

"10 Questions to Ask When Hiring an Attorney"
Free download at lisafraley.com/attorneyquestions ($197 value)

Chapter 7.

Trademark. Leadership. Crown Chakra.

I'm a Gemini (an air sign!), not to mention I'm a lawyer. Which means that I spend a LOT of time in my head. Thinking. Chatting. Producing. Growing up (and even today), my dad always said that he couldn't watch a TV show or movie with me because I'd ask a million questions. (When I got married, my dad said to my husband, "If you ever want to watch a show in peace, good luck with that!") My brain is always going. I regularly use running, yoga and meditation to slow my brain down, but it's not always easy. My natural state is to be in thought and motion.

I admit I've been called a "dizzy blonde" at times in my life. I've been called "Elle Woods." I've been called a "smarty-pants social butterfly."

If you're like me and you spend time floating around, dreaming up ideas, asking questions (especially during TV shows—ha!), you may not feel settled, grounded, or anchored either. When your head's up in the clouds, it can be difficult to center yourself in your life and business. But when you feel poised, aligned, and stable, you can be firmly planted while you're dreaming up the possibilities for your future.

The goal is to be rooted in your body, grounded in your purpose, solid in your business, and have a clear vision for your life and company—all at the same time.

Stand as a Leader in Your Business

As an entrepreneur, there's no doubt that we fill many roles all at once. We need to be the mate who drops the anchor, the navigator of the ship AND the captain at the helm. No matter how much help we receive from talented team members at the table, we're still responsible for holding the vision, setting the goals, managing the tasks AND ensuring it's all executed properly. As the owner of our businesses, the buck (literally and figuratively) stops—and starts—with us. From top to bottom, beginning to end.

When you're the leader of anything—a business, a family, a volunteer organization—you are generally the one who can see more of the landscape from a wide range of vantage points. Your view from the castle window allows you to survey your kingdom at a high level. As the queen (or king) of anything, it's your job to lead the way.

My first experience having this kind of wide perspective as a leader came when I was president and board chair of the Junior League of Portland.

I had been in leadership positions in organizations throughout my whole life—in high school as president of the Youth in Government, in college as president of my Delta Delta Delta sorority pledge class, and in law school as the managing editor of *Health Matrix: Journal of Law-Medicine*, so I had some experience and perspective in managing organizations.

But, the Junior League presidency was the first time I was truly challenged to hold the vision of the future of the organization while balancing day-to-day activities and members' concerns.

The Most Rewarding Charity Work I've Ever Done

I would be remiss if I didn't express my appreciation for the most rewarding charity work I've ever done as a decades-long member and as a past president of my local chapter of the Junior League.

210

What's the Junior League? If you haven't heard of it, it's "an organization of women committed to voluntarism, developing the potential of women, and improving the community through the effective action and leadership of trained volunteers. Its purpose is exclusively educational and charitable." The vision of the Junior League is to be "women around the world as catalysts for lasting community change." There are 150,000 women in 291 Junior League chapters all over the world, and I've belonged to the Junior League of Columbus (Ohio) and the Junior League of Portland (Maine).

I first joined the Junior League because I had moved to a new city and had heard it was a good way to make new friends with community-minded women - who also liked to do charitable fundraising and throw swanky parties. My grandmother had been a member of the Junior League of Columbus, and I had heard throughout my life how much she loved it, so I joined the same chapter as she had…fifty years later.

I learned fundraising techniques, leadership skills, board management, and I donated countless volunteer hours working with soup kitchens, food pantries, homeless shelters, youth programs, and literacy tutoring—not to mention, I made some of the closest friends of my life.

My two decades of membership, eight years of board service, and honor of serving as the president and board chair of my local Junior League by far has been the most rewarding charity work I've ever done, and it's been the most important personal growth experience of my life (that is, until I became an entrepreneur).

> If you're interested in connecting with women, volunteering your time, and improving the community, you can find more information about a Junior League near you at www.ajli.org.

When I was the president of the Junior League, one of the fundraising committees wanted to research, prepare, and publish a cookbook to raise money. Award-winning cookbooks have been published by Junior Leagues around the country for over 50 years, but the world had changed from the time of my grandmother's Junior League when cookbooks were a staple. Nowadays, people go online to purchase cookbooks or get free recipes at their fingertips. As beautiful and fun as they are, tangible, printed cookbooks have been going by the wayside as a key fundraising tool for non-profit organizations.

A dear friend of mine was the chair of the cookbook fundraising committee. During one of our one-on-one meetings, she passionately presented the arguments for publishing the League's third cookbook, along with her thorough research about financing, marketing, designing, editing, and publishing. There was a segment of League members who passionately wanted to publish another cookbook, as it had been part of the Junior League tradition for years to do so.

As harsh as it may sound, I wanted to nix the whole idea.

I saw the League going a different direction. I knew that the rapid evolution of digital media and technology would make it far more difficult to sell printed cookbooks today than it had been even 10 or 15 years ago. I wasn't sure why the committee didn't immediately see that as well, but sometimes when we're fervent about something, we see the upsides easily and downplay some of the negatives. It's totally normal.

I knew that I was going to have to publicly state that I opposed the idea—and that scared me.

I knew that I was going to be "the bad guy," and that felt extra hard because I was used to being "the good girl."

The League would be stepping outside of tradition by NOT printing the cookbook, and I knew that my decision wasn't going to be a popular one with some of the members. The final decision was a board decision—not mine alone—but my recommendation and opinion carried substantial weight, and I knew that it would.

Because I was the one perched at the top of the organization for my year-long term as president and board chair, I could see the entire landscape of the organization and the big picture. And as hard as it was, I just knew that it wasn't in the League's best interests to proceed with the cookbook.

Just as with any non-profit organization, the president and board chair is charged with protecting the interests of the ENTIRE organization—and not just parts of it—and it quickly became evident to me that no one else had a 360° view of the kingdom. I quickly discovered that it was my job as the president to make every decision from this perspective.

I felt a heavy sense of responsibility as the president, not to mention that as the board chair, I also had the legal duties of loyalty and care to do what was in the best interest of the organization.

That's Why They Say "It's Lonely at the Top"

For the first time, I realized what a lonely, scary, isolating experience it can be as the "top" of anything.

(And heck, I was just the president of the Junior League—I cannot even imagine how it would feel to be the President of the United States. An unbelievable position, no matter who sits in that chair.)

I knew I had to make a recommendation based on what was best for the long-term future of our local League.

I knew that by making a decision, I would disappoint people.

I knew that people would talk about me behind my back and that I'd risk not being well-liked by some members for the decision ... and that killed me inside.

But, standing as I was in the position of being the only one who could see across the entire organization, I also knew it was the right decision to make. And so I made it.

I politely and respectfully showed gratitude and respect to the committee for their hard work, and I shared why I didn't believe that publishing a cookbook was in the League's best interest at that time.

My dear friend–the committee chair––was angry with me. She felt personally let down by me and upset that her idea would not be brought to fruition after working on it and researching it for months and months.

Her committee was disappointed and frustrated. I felt some of the members distance themselves from me. But I knew that my loyalty had to be to the larger vision, to the role that was expected of me, and I had to honor the decision-making that comes from being the only one who stands at the top of the mountain and sees every part of the landscape. It was my job to lead the way and to wear the crown ... just like it's yours in your business.

It was one of the hardest decisions I had ever made.

It was one of the first times I had said no in such a public and large scale way and risked disappointing people I cared about.

Although it was a professional decision and I was well-liked by most League members, I took it to heart, and the negative ramifications from some of the members felt personal.

But, I knew I had to wear the crown as the leader, and with that responsibility comes the challenge of stepping up to make difficult decisions.

You're Expected to Wear the Crown

You'll never guess what happened after I made that difficult Junior League decision to speak out and share my unpopular opinion.

A few years later, that same dear friend who had been the committee chair had risen to the role of president of the Junior League. She came up to me at an event and said: "Lisa, I am so sorry. I totally get it now. When I was the committee chair, I didn't know what it was like to be the one responsible for the whole organization, not just what one committee wants or desires. You made the right decision to not go forward with the cookbook when you were the president. I didn't realize at the time that you're the only one who can see the whole landscape and you're charged with protecting the entire organization's best interests. I just had no idea."

As you can imagine, her confession surprised me, but it was incredibly healing for me. I had followed what I knew to be right and true at the time—the Right Path—but it had been hard.

I don't share this story to emphasize that she told me I had made the "correct" or "accurate" decision – that's not the point. I share this story to show how when you are the leader of an organization—the queen of your business—it's up to you to make "right" and "true" decisions that are in the best interest of your organization, which are often the hard and courageous decisions. Your job is to do it. You're expected to do it. Your role is to wear the crown.

It's Hard to Say No

In holding the vision for the life and business that you want, you need to figure out when to say "yes" to opportunities that are aligned with your goals, and when to say "no" to the people, offers, partnerships or anything else that isn't lined up with your vision or that's not in the best interest of your business.

Your job is to say "yes" to your deepest, heart-centered desires, and "no" to something that doesn't feel aligned. And that, my friend, is not easy.

It's hard to say "no."

It's hard to worry that you won't be liked if you turn down requests to speak on stage, be part of online summits, or go out to lunch with your friends because you need to focus on your launch, dig out from client work, or stay home and write a chapter of your upcoming book. (Who me?)

It's hard to stand in your power and share a truthful opinion or insight when you know it might meet resistance or trigger someone else's negative reaction.

It's scary to worry that you won't be liked for not being available to your clients 24/7—or that if you don't take calls during nights or weekends that clients will get mad and go look for someone else.

It takes courage to show up and wonder if you will be disliked, diminished or disregarded.

If your head's in the clouds and you find yourself often feeling murky or airy-fairy, it's even harder. When you don't feel grounded, it's challenging to stay anchored while you're navigating new waters and making important decisions that affect your income and your life.

Just like a boat on the open sea, if you don't drop an anchor, you'll end up off course without even noticing it until your boat drifts onto a beach in a place you don't recognize. That's not a good feeling. Blowing adrift and running amok are not ideal for boats or business owners.

Taking the right path and showing up as a leader in your business is essential, especially if you're the only one who can see the full landscape.

Legal Superpowers Give You Grace

Legal documents empower you to stand tall in your role as the king or queen of your business—and give you special superpowers.

When you have strong legal documents for your biz, you don't have to feel guilty for wanting to draw lines and establish expectations as the ruler of your business. You can honor your written policies and boundaries with greater ease when they are in writing and all spelled out, and that gives you the confidence and security you need when you're reigning over your business.

Legal documents give you extra superpowers...like grace. Legal documents give you the power to say "no" while staying emotionally neutral in a trying situation. Legal documents allow you to respond to conflicts with your head held high with grace.

With your documents backing you, you don't have to get sucked into the drama with a client. You can respond rationally.

Having your work content stolen or your policies questioned can feel so emotionally raw and personal, so falling back on your legal documents helps you to remain neutral and in control. If you suddenly receive an e-mail from a panicked client who is in a tizzy, you don't have to absorb that energy or get drawn into the tizzy yourself. You can remain neutral, safe, and comfortable and turn to your documents for grounded support.

Knowing your documents already have your policies spelled out in writing, you give yourself the time and space to compose your thoughts and emotions before you respond to your tizzy client. You know you have legal support at your back, and it allows you to relax and deepen into your power and authority.

Here's an example:

My client Alexa told me one day that she felt instantly empowered after taking my "get legally covered so you can go bare" course. Through the course, she prepared her Client Agreement, Website Disclaimer, Website Terms & Conditions and Terms of Use and got clear about the policies of her business. When a client asked for refund for a program with a no-refund policy, she told me she felt comfortable firmly and lovingly holding her ground by saying simply, "The Terms of Use for my group program has a no-refund policy, which you agreed to when you signed up at the start of the course, and that's the policy of my business."

It's the Policy of My Business

For Alexa, it was easy to stand behind the clarity of her position and policy because it was a consistent business policy that she was honoring, after creating it with foresight and care.

It wasn't a personal decision to deny her client a refund. It was the loving policy of her business.

Alexa's legal documents reflected the values and principles that she wanted to present to the world through her business as being fair, loving, and kind, but also clear, strong and consistent. It made the conversation with her client so much more comfortable, clear, and empowering knowing she was only honoring a policy of her business; it wasn't personal.

Alexa didn't have to get into a back and forth emotional conversation with her client. Her policy was spelled out in writing, and she could easily refer the client to the section where the policy was stated.

Alexa could respond with dignity, integrity, power and ease—and the way she responded to her client was important. She could stand as the queen of her business and share her policies without inner conflict or struggle wondering if she was making the right choice.

She didn't need to second-guess herself or wonder if she wasn't being kind or sensitive to the client. She knew that she could have overridden her contractual terms and given the client a full refund if she felt so moved, but she didn't feel the situation called for it.

Alexa felt that enforcing her no-refund policy was the right decision, and her legal document made it easy to express that decision, with no fear or anxiety on her part.

That's the whole idea.

Legal documents (and lawyers!) are your friends who are here to help you feel empowered, strong, protected, and powerful in your business.

Your legal documents exist solely to support and bolster your business.

It doesn't matter how new or seasoned you may be, it can feel a little scary each time you step up and into your power in a bigger way. It can feel like a stretch to wear your business crown with confidence.

But when you have your agreements, disclaimers, and intellectual property protections in place, being the leader of your business becomes a whole lot easier.

Just like the king or queen, when you have your decrees in writing, you get to be the decision-maker as to how you want your work to be treated and used.

In fact, everyone you work with, including clients, partners, team members, and peers, expect you to show up, stand tall, enforce boundaries, and act like a leader. If you don't wear the crown as the queen of your business, that's the time when you'll be letting people down. They expect you to be the leader of your business and the CEO of your company. They WANT you to do it. Your job is to do it. It's expected – and that can give you some comfort.

It's Time to Recognize Yourself as the Queen (or King)

Over time, as you step forward and step up in your biz as the leader of your tribe, you get more comfortable sharing your message with your unique twist, hosting your own webinars and masterminds, leading your own group courses and becoming more comfortable with the attention, visibility, and vulnerability that comes with expanding your business.

At the same time, as you become shinier, bigger, and more visible, other people may try to emulate and copy you and your brand as well. We've already talked about those who copy your website content (Chapter 4) and

219

your group programs, online courses, products and content (Chapter 5) and now we'll address Copycats and Swipers who are trying to pilfer your branding by using your logo, business name, program name, or tagline.

It can feel defeating when you've tirelessly worked to build a unique brand with your own clever tagline and a logo that you absolutely adore, and you turn on your computer one day, click on someone's Facebook post promoting their new website, and see your title, content, ideas—even the exact words that you created—showing up on someone else's site, especially when you've trademarked them.

Copycats and Swipers try to copy your logo or tagline because they want what you have—the success, ease, comfort, lifestyle, and financial earnings that you have. They want it for themselves.

In Chapter 5, we talked about first presuming innocence if you think that someone's ripped off your program or product, but invariably, there are business owners out there who aren't innocent and who knowingly steal your tagline or program name, change a word here or there, then try to claim their name is their original creation.

Just like when parts of your website or program guide are copied or swiped, it feels awful when your branding is stolen too. It's infuriating, discouraging, and frustrating. It can feel disempowering and violating that someone disrespected your business so much that they tried to directly benefit from your brand identity.

Those are the kinds of Copycats and Swipers who don't come from a heart-centered place—even if they say on their website that they do. They're self-centered "warriors," and you need to be wary of them. They may push back and argue with you, but in their core, they know they're trying to take something that they know you created or used before they did, and they're trying to benefit and profit from your good work and goodwill. Some part of them is not in ethical integrity, or they wouldn't have knowingly tried to piggyback on your success. Not only should they be disgusted with themselves for stealing (even if they're in self-denial about what they did), but rest assured, deep inside there's a part of themselves that knows the truth about their actions and how insecure they are that they can't even stand on their own two feet.

You are wise to put into place as many legal protections as you can to protect your brand, and that includes protecting your intellectual property through using legal protections like trademarks.

Ownership of Ideas and the Collective Consciousness

Before we dive into trademarks and touch on intellectual property, I've heard some say that they believe that ideas belong to all of us. That no one can own an idea or a concept because ideas all come from collective consciousness, and therefore no one person can claim that he or she truly "owns" an idea.

The argument goes that few ideas are truly original, and for the most part, new concepts are really just built on ideas that have preceded them, and all that's been added is a unique spin or minor tweaks or details. In many ways, this theory is true. Ideas themselves are not allowed to be owned. Ideas float around in the collective consciousness, accessible to all and belonging to no one.

However, there's a difference between *ideas*, which belong to all of us collectively, and the *creative expression of those ideas*, which are attributed to us individually.

Intellectual property law permits an individual or company to own and protect the *creative expression* of ideas.

When ideas are expressed in writing or through film, in music, or any other form of media or communication, ownership and intellectual property rights may be attached to the unique expression of those ideas.

Governments from all over the world have established laws, rules, and ordinances that protect the property and rights of others. Property includes tangible and intangible property, extending to and including intellectual property which covers the expression of creative ideas. Recognition of creative ideas as property is the basis for laws allowing copyrights, trademarks, and patents to be issued. Under local, state, and federal laws and government protection, individuals are legally allowed to own the *expression* of ideas as assets and may financially benefit from their use and prevent others from benefitting from their owned assets.

So even if it's true that ideas may be created and improved upon through the collective consciousness as information, knowledge, experience evolves as a human global society, the creative tools used to communicate those ideas to the world—such as books, articles, artwork, photographs, movies, logos, etc.—are given specific protections under the law.

You are allowed to claim your intellectual property and ownership rights as they are granted to you, and you may enforce your rights if someone violates them.

If a Copycat or Swiper steals your stuff and you're feeling disempowered, it's hard to feel like a leader of your business.

You may feel confused, anxious, angry, and helpless—all at the same time. You may feel like things are happening TO you and your business without your permission and control, instead of you standing at the helm and steering your ship.

You may feel like the farthest thing from the king or queen of your business and that you've lost control of the kingdom.

You may not be sure how to course-correct or where to find your power and confidence.

(Flip back to Chapter 3 on confidence to regain your power.)

When you encounter a Copycat or Swiper, you might be wondering, "But, can they just copy whatever they want if it's not copyrighted or trademarked?" Do you have to sit in silence looking at YOUR branding on THEIR website while your rage is growing and you're about to explode?

The answer is no.

You Can Fight Back Against Copycats and Swipers

When Copycats and Swipers steal your images, taglines and titles without your permission, you don't have to sit in silence.

If you DO have Trademarks and Copyrights, you can assert your intellectual property rights. If you have a registered Copyright or Trademark, you can take action based on Copyright or Trademark infringement, respectively.

If you DON'T have a registered Copyright or Trademark, you can use your legal documents like your Client Agreement, Website Terms & Conditions and/or Terms of Use for Online Programs and Products to support you and give you the backing you need to claim breach of contractual terms, and you have the necessary language to support your position. (That's one of the many reasons why ALL these documents are so important to have in your legal toolbox.)

As we talked about in Chapter 5, you also can send—or have a lawyer send—a Cease and Desist Letter to require that the Swiper "cease" their actions and demand that they stop using your logo or tagline by a certain date or you'll pursue further legal action.

Just like with your website, programs and products, you want to be clear as to where you draw your lines when it comes to others using your logo, branding, taglines, titles and business name, and using legal documents and intellectual property protections like Trademarks and Copyrights can help.

Can you now see how what we've discussed in each chapter is all coming together to protect your work and give you a strong legal foundation? You just put the easy legal steps in place one step at a time.

In this chapter, we're going to focus on the last of the seven key legal protections and that's how to Trademark.

Your Legal Step: Trademark

Obtaining a Trademark is the crown jewel for a small business owner or entrepreneur.

When you are the king or queen of your business, not only does it feel good wearing the crown, but it feels good having a crowning achievement. Receiving a Trademark for your business name, logo, or tagline gives you supreme federal protection along with peace of mind and confidence that you're protecting your brand.

Your brand is the descriptive representation of your values, your vision, your mission, and your passion. It's the way you express to the world who you are and what you stand for. It's infused with your intentions, awareness, energy, and emotion—whether you realize it or not.

Your brand contains both the practical and spiritual components of what you present and represent to the world, and you are permitted to protect it and keep it safe.

The whole point of Trademarking is to receive federal statutory protection to use a few words or a logo related to your brand in a certain context, and to keep others from benefitting from your branding identity, market recognition and goodwill by using the same or similar words or logo in a comparable field.

The purpose of Trademarking is to protect your brand recognition and to keep two unrelated brands from being confused by consumers.

It's also designed to prevent other business owners from financially benefitting from your hard-earned brand identity and value in the marketplace.

What Can You Trademark and Why Should You Do It?

Simply put, Trademarks are used for words, phrases, symbols, designs, or graphics. (To find out if you have something that is worth trademarking, check out "How Do You Know What's Trademark-Worthy?" Assessment in the Legal Love™ Bonus Content at the end of this chapter.)

Trademarks are used for shorter phrases or word combinations or for symbols or graphics like a logo versus Copyrights which are used for longer creative works to protect original authorship. (See box below.)

The US Patent and Trademark Office (USPTO), which is the government office which oversees the Trademarking process, allows you to Trademark a unique combination of words or logo, provided there isn't a "likelihood of confusion" with an existing Trademark (also referred to as a "mark" for short.)

A Trademark is granted under federal law to give you the exclusive right to use your words or logo in a particular Trademark class. It prevents others doing similar work in a similar field from using words or graphics that are the same or "substantially similar" to yours.

The USPTO allows you to apply for federal Trademark protection of your program name, business name, taglines, titles, logo, and more, provided the USPTO examiner reviews how you are using your brand in the marketplace and concludes there's no likelihood of confusion with an existing mark that's already been approved.

What About Copyright?

Business owners often confuse Trademarks and Copyrights. Trademarks and Copyrights are entirely different intellectual protections overseen by different government offices and granted under separate federal statutes.

It helps to think of them like cousins in intellectual property (along with their third cousin - Patents), but they aren't siblings. Trademarks and Copyrights follow different rules and they have different "parent" offices who create them, oversee them and monitor their bedtimes.

Federal Copyrights are granted under the US Copyright Act and overseen by the US Copyright Office. Their purpose is to protect the authorship of original creative works.

The easiest way to distinguish Copyrights from Trademarks is that Copyrights are generally used for longer artistic or literary works or an entire body of work, and Trademarks are just for short phrases and logos used in branding.

Copyright protection is extended to a wide variety of items, like books, articles, poems, movies, sound recordings, screenplays, photographs, jewelry designs, or artwork – basically, creative works that people develop that they don't want anyone to copy without their consent.

When you create a work, it's true that your work is under Copyright once it is created and "fixed in a tangible form" – in other words, once it's memorialized in a permanent form that isn't going to change. Your right in the work is established the moment the final version is completed.

HOWEVER, you don't have legal protection of your work such that you could bring a lawsuit or stop someone else from using your work unless you voluntarily file for Copyright registration with the US Copyright Office to obtain the protection of the US Copyright laws.

In other words, when you've written a book, you typically don't go in and change the book text after its been published or edit the song lyrics after the song's been played on the radio. Copyrights protect what's approved in the application EXACTLY as is, so a new Copyright must be obtained for any future editions of the book or renditions of the song with substantive changes. This is why when you open a book cover, you'll see a "2nd edition" or "3rd edition" of a book with different Copyright dates than the original publication date. A new Copyright had to be sought and granted for subsequent editions of the book.

Many small businesses with an online presence wonder if they should Copyright blog posts or program guides, but entrepreneurs are known for editing website text, adding blog posts, and updating program guides all the time. If you want to Copyright a blog or website or program guide but make more than a few minor edits to it, the new edits won't be protected by the Copyright – only the original text – so it's not usually ideal to Copyright unless you file updates to the original application or even a new application.

As an entrepreneur, you can see why filing for a Copyright isn't often recommended.

For that reason, while Copyrighting is an important legal protection, it's not often used by entrepreneurs unless they write a book or they're an artist, photographer or jewelry designer.

Hence, I don the Trademark as the crowning achievement for small business owners and entrepreneurs and have aligned it with the crown chakra since more biz owners seek Trademarks to protect and honor their brand than Copyrights or even Patents.

Don't Let Someone Beat You to the Punch

One of the biggest fears that my clients share is that when they've developed a business name, tagline, program name or logo that they absolutely love, they worry that someone else will take it and use it—or will beat them to the punch in using it.

If you can make a lot of money with your creative biz name or tagline, you're wise to protect it now before someone else snags it. Don't risk waiting for someone else to Trademark the same or similar idea. If you wait, you may lose out or have to fight for it—it happens all the time.

Trademarking is a long process. It can take 6-18 months and averages about 10-12 months. It's a significant investment of time, energy, and money because it's a process with many steps between starting with an idea and getting a Trademark granted.

Getting a Trademark isn't ever guaranteed. But it's totally worth it if it's granted to you, because you get legal rights to your mark for ten years—a small price to pay for a large return on your investment – and you can renew your mark for subsequent ten-year periods.

At first glance, Trademarking looks super-easy, but it's actually quite tricky.

Trademarking is a 2-step process.

Step 1—The Trademark Search

The first step is to have a lawyer conduct a Trademark Search to make sure that the word, phrase or graphic you want to Trademark is available, and that you're not going to be treading on someone else's existing mark.

Let's look at Penelope as an example. Penelope's a yoga instructor. She's opening up a new yoga studio and wants to call it "Peace and Calm Yoga Studio." Like a lot of business owners, Penelope heard that she could look up the USPTO Trademark database online to see if the name she wants to Trademark is already taken. Penelope sat down at her laptop and typed in "Peace and Grace Yoga Studio" into the database. Much to Penelope's excitement, she was thrilled when she saw that no other results popped up with "Peace and Grace" in them. It appeared as if the name wasn't taken. She felt elated and proceeded to file her Trademark Application on her own.

Often, when entrepreneurs like Penelope do a cursory search, they see that nothing is already Trademarked with the exact words they desire and they think the coast is clear to file a Trademark Application and sail through the process with ease. However, they receive a rude awakening—just like Penelope did—when they later learn that their Trademark is denied based on a conflict with an existing mark.

In Penelope's case, she called me one day and said, "But, Lisa, I don't understand. I looked in the USPTO database and there wasn't anything with the same name. No other results came up with those same exact words. I saw something for "Graceful Lines & Peaceful Poses" but that was for a ballet studio and I'm a yoga instructor."

WHAM.

It's not enough to do a quick check in the USPTO database to see if your phrase is already Trademarked. That's a good initial step, but you can't stop there.

If Penelope had invested in a formal Trademark Search with a lawyer, it would have been easy for the lawyer to see the other result that came up for "Graceful Lines & Peaceful Poses" posed a potential conflict because it was for a business that also dealt with physical movement of the body and the mark was filed in the same Trademark class. Ugh!

A formal Trademark Search conducted by a lawyer can help estimate the level or risk there is to proceed with a Trademark Application. The lawyer's assessment will be based not only on whether there are marks that are exactly the same, but whether other marks exist that aren't exactly the same but that are similar-sounding enough to stop your mark from going forward in a particular Trademark class.

As you can see from Penelope's example, having a lawyer who understands the legal lens through which the USPTO will view your words, phrase or logo do a formal Trademark Search can save you a ton of time, energy, and money later. Lawyers familiar with intellectual property law are trained to discern potential conflicts and share this information with you BEFORE you file a Trademark Application, rather than after you've spent time and money submitting the Application and it doesn't get approved.

Because so much work is done on the front end to prepare a Trademark Application, the government (and most lawyers) don't give refunds if the Trademark isn't granted. The small investment in the Trademark Search is worth every penny.

After I explained why the USPTO had denied her mark, Penelope told me she wished she'd just invested a few hundred dollars in the Trademark Search right from the start. She said she wouldn't make that same mistake ever again.

A lot of small business owners who file Trademark Applications on their own miss this first Trademark Search step and later wonder why the USPTO denied their mark. They don't understand that had they invested in the Trademark Search, a lawyer would have given them a legal analysis of what would be perceived as a conflict and advised the business owner whether or not to proceed with a Trademark Application accordingly.

There are many legal steps where you can use DIY legal templates or file local documents on your own, but conducting a Trademark Search is one where it is strongly recommended that you receive legal help. Intellectual property law is a specialized area, even for lawyers. It can appear easy but it's far more complex than most might think.

The Trademark Search is a critical step – don't skip it.

Step 2—The Trademark Application

After you've had the Trademark Search, preferably conducted by a lawyer, your next step is to file a Trademark Application. The Trademark Application requires precision, attention, accuracy and responsiveness, especially around the language used for your description and the selection of your Trademark classes. Again, it's wise to seek legal help so you don't provide the wrong information, choose the wrong Trademark class, or leave room for someone to sneak in the back door because your wording didn't fully cover you.

There are two approaches to filing a Trademark Application with the USPTO:

- In Use - once your mark is already "in use in commerce"

- Intent to Use - if you have the "intent to use" it in your branding in commerce in the next six months (though you can file numerous extensions.)

It's easier and less expensive to file a Trademark Application with the "In Use" designation AFTER you've been using the word, phrase, logo or design in your business.

The whole point of a Trademark is to protect the brand identity, financial value, intellectual property, and intangible rights (like

231

goodwill) that you've generated in your word, phrase or logo in the marketplace.

Thus, to be granted a Trademark registration for a mark that is "In Use," you must be using the mark in business and earning income with it; you can't Trademark it for just a hobby.

However, because the USPTO recognizes that sometimes businesses want to claim the word, phrase, logo or design BEFORE they build out their website or complete their construction of their brick-and-mortar shop, the USPTO lets you file in a category that recognizes your "Intent to Use" the mark. You still must provide information to show your mark is being used in commerce for the Trademark to be granted, but you can buy yourself some lead time before you have to submit samples of your use to the USPTO.

When you submit a Trademark Application, you must fill out a form and also submit compelling samples – often called "proof of use" or "specimens" to the USPTO as to how you are using the words, phrase, or log that you'd like to Trademark. You need to follow the deadlines for each step of the lengthy process and respond to any requests for clarification by the USPTO presented in formal Office Actions. Your lawyer can also handle the communication and back and forth with the USPTO, which can be confusing, and make arguments on your behalf if you need to clarify your use of the words or defend your position.

When it comes to the Trademark Application assuring that you have a precise Trademark description about how you use the mark relative to your goods or services and identifying the right Trademark classes are two critical steps that can make or break an Application.

- The Trademark description needs to be thorough and accurate and written in a way that prevents others with similar services from filing a similar mark.

- The Trademark classes, of which there are 45, are the categories into which you want your mark to fall, and strategically determining which classes are appropriate for your mark is an integral step of the process that is key to your success.

As with the Trademark Search, preparing and filing the Trademark Application is a key step where you'll want to get legal help. It may look straightforward, but I can't tell you how many clients have come to me for assistance after they tried to file a mark on their own. Trademarking is nuanced and is a specialized area of the law requiring experience and expertise. Don't go it alone.

Let me give you an example of a Trademark experience gone wrong so you can see why getting legal help is so important right from the start—and, boy, did it go wrong!

Oprah, an Entrepreneur, and a Trademark Walk into a Courtroom

This a true life scenario. It was a real court case. I wasn't involved in any part of the legal battle, but I want to share it to quickly show you how powerful a federal Trademark can be—and what can happen if it isn't done properly and thoroughly.

Meet Simone. Simone is a coach and owner of Own Your Power Communications, Inc.

Back in 2007, Simone trademarked the words "Own Your Power®" as a part of her business.

It was a wise move by a smart entrepreneur to invest in her work and protect the heart of her brand.

Then along comes Oprah.

Oprah puts the words "Own Your Power" smack on the October 2010 cover of Oprah magazine.

It's not surprising that Simone believed that Oprah's use of the words violated her trademark rights. After all, Oprah used the EXACT words that she had trademarked over three years prior.

Here's how it went down:

Simone sues Oprah for violating her registered Trademark ... and Oprah wins.

Wait -WHAT?! How did that happen?

I mean, we all know she's Oprah! But seriously, how did she win?

The whole point of Trademarking is to give you the rights to use words in a particular context, and to stop others from using them in a similar or substantially similar way.

If Simone had a registered Trademark, how could Oprah have won the case? She didn't win just because she's Oprah (believe it or not), but because Simone's Trademark Application description wasn't written in an ironclad way and Oprah snuck in the back door.

What does that mean exactly? Let me explain.

There are three basic reasons why the judge ruled for Oprah and not for Simone (and I am generously summarizing here):[24]

Reason #1: The judge said that Simone's trademark description of "Own Your Power®" wasn't "distinctive" enough.

Basically, the description that Simone used in her Trademark Application wasn't written in a way that was descriptive enough to prevent someone else in a similar field from also using it. And because the description wasn't specific enough, there was room for Oprah to slide in alongside her. The exact words you use in your Trademark Application are critically important. You want to be sure your choice of words are precise and descriptive. (This is where the help of a lawyer comes in.)

Reason #2: The judge said that Simone hadn't provided enough proof to show that "Own Your Power®" was widely recognizable as a part of her brand.

Again, I'm paraphrasing here to make this legal info easier to digest, but the judge basically said that Simone hadn't included enough evidence of advertising, media coverage or other support showing that "Own Your Power®" was indispensable and recognizable as the basis of Simone's brand. Simone needed to show more evidence to show that people immediately associated "Own Your Power®" with Simone and her business.

Reason #3: The judge ruled that there was no "likelihood of confusion" between the two brands.

In general, when you file a Trademark infringement case, you are basically saying that someone violated your Trademark in a way that causes a "likelihood of confusion" between your brand and another, and that people will mix up your brands, which devalues your intellectual property. The goal is to have no "likelihood of confusion" between your brand and someone else's brand. The judge ruled in this case that it wasn't super-likely that people would confuse Simone's brand with Oprah's. Not surprising, right?

I don't know of ANYONE whose brand could be confused with Oprah's. She totally stands in a league of her own. Her notoriety notwithstanding, the judge found that Simone hadn't established her own use of Own Your Power® in a substantive enough way for it to be a uniquely identifiable part of her brand.

So that's what happened. And that's why Oprah won.

But you know what's MOST interesting of all to me? The case was over the words "Own Your Power®."

Own Your Power

Own your power. Isn't that ironic? Owning your dreams, your desires, and your power are themes that have been repeated throughout this book because of how important it is to "own your power" in your business.

For certain, Simone sure owned her power when she stood up to Oprah. Not many people would have the courage or gumption to sue Oprah for a Trademark infringement.

I haven't shared all the details of the litigation here (because it was a long legal process), but Simone actually first brought her case in federal court, then it went up to the 2nd Circuit Court of Appeals, and then the case was sent back to the lower court where the decision was made in Oprah's favor. Then Simone appealed again to the 2nd Circuit Court of Appeals, and again the case was awarded in Oprah's favor. WHEW!

Amazing, right? Simone endured four rounds of court battles to fight for her rights. Four rounds! Simone CERTAINLY owned every ounce of her power and I respect her strength to endure that much litigation and to take one of the most powerful business owners in the world.

Is It Even Worth It to Trademark?

After reading about Simone's case, you may be wondering, "So, is it even worth it to Trademark when I may not even win in a dispute?" Let me reassure you, the answer is a resounding YES. Despite the risks, it's worth every dollar.

Trademarks protect you immensely.

I myself have two Trademarks—for Legal Coach® and Holistic Lawyer®. They are key protections for my brand identity and honor the work, energy and conscious thought I've put into my brand. Likewise, your brand has tremendous value. You want to protect it.

Trademark disputes depend on multiple factors, but they often hinge on Trademark Application descriptions – just like in Simone's case. So, if you remember NOTHING else about Trademarks, remember this: Your Trademark description needs to be spot-on and really specific, or it may have holes that can be left open for the likes of Oprah or other challengers.

Professional expertise is highly recommended. I'm not kidding when I say that it's ill-advised to Trademark alone. I am not kidding when I say that I recommend that you have an experienced Trademark lawyer to help you. As I've mentioned, the Trademark process looks easy and straightforward at first glance, but it can really be tricky.

Trademark is the Crown Jewel

Trademark protection is about owning your power and wearing the crown.

Trademarking is one of the highest legal rights that can be given to you as a business leader to protect your unique, creative work. It's the crown jewel.

When it comes to obtaining one of the highest levels of legal protections you can receive as an entrepreneur, you'll want to make sure you do it correctly so you can protect yourself, your business, and your brand and stand as the powerful king or queen of your business.

Leadership and Trademarks Align with the Crown Chakra

Trademarking is such a high-frequency right that I align it with your crown chakra which correlates with your highest potential.

The crown chakra is called *Sahaswara* in Sanskrit, which translates to the "thousand petal" lotus flower, meaning that through the crown chakra we open to enlightenment and spiritual connection like the petals of a lotus flower open to the beauty that surrounds it.

The crown chakra is represented by the color of purple and is connected to your highest potential, wisdom, divinity, awareness, connection, freedom, and a calm state of being.

Trademarks are one of the ways that you connect your brand to something larger than you—the greater marketplace—and you create a legacy associated with your business.

Though Trademark registration lasts for ten years, you can renew it over again, providing you are still using it in your business and that you comply with the USPTO requirements for renewal, so your protection can expand indefinitely.

Trademarks can help you wear the crown of your business at your highest potential by owning the intellectual property rights to your tagline, logo, business or program name.

There will be moments – or days – when you don't feel like a leader and you need a reminder that the work you are doing is important, you can turn to this Crown Chakra Mantra to connect with something bigger and to remind you that you are wise and your brand has value.

Crown Chakra Mantra

When you are seeking more leadership and power to wear the crown in your life or business,
you can set your intention using this Crown Chakra mantra:

"I am connected. I am aware. I am present. I am wise."

There may be days where your Ego may get the best of you and you may not feel like you are far enough along in your business to consider yourself a leader. You may be thinking, "Lisa, I really don't feel like a leader of my business. There are so many gurus out there with million-dollar businesses—*they're* the ones who are the leaders. Why would people listen to me and not to them? What do I possibly have to offer that can compete with that kind of leadership?"

I get why you might feel that way. It's easy to fall into this line of thinking. It's easy to doubt yourself and your incredible talent and knowledge or that people might be drawn to you more than the Well-Known Gurus. It's easy to think that you won't be chosen and that others will work with someone else with more experience, expertise, or energy. We all feel that way sometimes.

You may doubt your leadership and value because you simply haven't seen enough proof of your success yet. Because once you see proof, you won't doubt it anymore.

Once you've received gleaming, sparkling testimonials from client after client after client, you'll be more able to recognize your value and your knowledge. You'll see yourself through the eyes of how other people see you, and know that you are helping them change their lives or their businesses, and that is validating.

When you're just starting out, you choose to model more established business owners and want to do things the way that they do it. Obviously, they've figured something out to have a multi-six figure business or a million-dollar business, that's for sure.

You may want to follow their rules, build your courses based on their "proven ways," and launch your course on their suggested timelines—and that's okay. You need to start somewhere. Following what coaches or entrepreneurs with more experience teach through their programs or courses is a great place to start.

After a while, when you've found your groove and you're clear on your ideal client, your mission and your message, you'll begin to tweak the models and formulas and do things in ways that feels right to you- and that's okay. In fact, I'd argue that it's exactly what you should be doing. Exactly.

Key Takeaways from This Chapter

With time, you find your own voice—and with it, the courage to be viewed as a leader in your own right. You'll develop your own unique program name, tagline or biz name, and you'll likely want to Trademark it and obtain those crowning rights.

Right now, keep moving in that direction. Every day you are getting closer and closer to the life and business you most want, business step by business step, and legal step by legal step.

Your seventh legal step is to Trademark.

Your seventh soul-centered principle is leadership.

Your chakra that is supported and aligned is your crown chakra.

Now It's Your Turn ...

Use this Legal Checklist and Business Self-Assessment to help you honor your brand, your power, and your leadership position standing as the queen (or king) of your business.

Legal Checklist:

1. Do you have a registered Trademark? (If so, you get a gold star!)

2. Have you ever had a Copycat or Swiper take or copy your brand or logo?

3. Do you have your legal documents in place to protect against Copycats and Swipers? (If so, you get another gold star!)

4. Have you responded calmly in a conflict with a client because you knew your legal documents stated your policies and you didn't have to get drawn into a drama?

5. Do you have something to Trademark? If you haven't gotten your Trademark yet, have you identified what's holding you back?

Business Self-Assessment:

1. Do you feel like you're the queen (or king) of your business?

2. Do you have a hard time saying no when it might disappoint others? (See how this is a recurring theme for most heart-centered entrepreneurs?)

3. Do you own your power?

4. Does having power or being a leader scare you or even make you a little uncomfortable?

Don't forget to grab your Legal Love™ Bonus Content!

Legal Love™ Bonus Content:

"How Do You Know What's Trademark-Worthy?" Assessment will help
find out if you have a name, tagline or logo that's worth trademarking.
Free download at lisafraley.com/diytrademarkassessment
($147 value - Use code WORTHY)

Going Forward

Deep down, I suspect you already know what you want for the next phase of your life and business. Even if the details are a bit fuzzy, I'm guessing you can envision at least snippets of the lifestyle you want in 5 years and the ways in which you want to help your tribe right now.

Even if you're still learning to tap into your intuition or to speak your voice with courage and confidence, you know enough about yourself to know when something feels good—and you are tuned in enough to sense when it's not aligned. You know what feels congruent with your mission - and what's not a match. You're schooled in your area of expertise, even if it feels like you're in a crowded marketplace or you're hesitant to call yourself an "experiential expert" yet.

How do I know this? Because I've worked with hundreds of business owners and if you were drawn to this book, I know you're well on your way to having the life and business of your dreams–regardless if you've been in business for a week or a decade.

Something inside you prompted you to learn about these seven easy legal steps, soul-aligned principles and chakras to raise your knowledge and professionalism, and up your biz vibe. You may have been intrigued by the legal and spiritual connection or my lawyer/coach cross-training combo, but I hope you recognize that you too can bring all of your gifts together into your business and create your own unique brand.

You're already an expert and a leader, and no one can better teach and guide others from your perspective than you can.

No one has your history, your creativity, your special twist on your knowledge, your experiential expertise, or your leadership.

Know that I see you and recognize you – and that I'm cheering you on.

As each chapter has explored, you now know that legal documents help you feel protected and bolstered as a leader of your business. Throughout this book:

- You've seen the importance of a **Website Disclaimer** as a base layer of legal protection to ground and protect you as you clearly disclaim your liability when you vulnerably launch (or relaunch) your website.

- You've learned that I like to call legal documents "compassionate containers" and gifts to both you and your clients. You now know that as you outline crystal clear policies in your **Client Agreement**, you'll have far fewer requests for refunds or issues with non-payment with one-on-one clients. Your income and boundaries will be more secure and protected.

- You've seen that as you get clear on **Business Registration and Taxes as a Sole Proprietor** and as you go pro by tapping into your intuition and filing a **LLC or S-Corp**, you elevate your professionalism which makes everyone around you – including yourself – take your business more seriously.

- You've learned that as you protect your website with your **Website Terms and Conditions** and keep your visitors' info safe with a **Privacy Policy**, you're plugging energy leaks and courageously drawing lines so Copycats and Swipers will be less likely to sneak in and copy your website content.

- You've also watched how having your group program, online course, or product purchasers agree to your **Terms of Use** can create smooth online business transactions, reduce headaches and conflicts over payment, and establish firm guidelines around how your program or products can be used by the purchaser.

- And, you've seen how you can secure your intellectual property rights to a business name or tagline to protect your brand identity and value with federal **Trademark** registration.

Not only that, but you've seen how the relationship between clarity and the root chakra, boundaries and the sacral chakra, confidence and the solar plexus chakra, courage and the heart chakra, communication and the throat chakra, intuition and the third eye chakra, and leadership and the crown chakra can help you succeed in business through an understanding of seven soul-centered principles and energy centers that can fuel you both on a practical level and a spiritual level.

The whole purpose of this book is to help you know how to get legally covered, so you can expand and share your gifts with the world in an even bigger way. I wanted to show you how feeling safe and secure in your business allows you to feel confident and empowered to bare your heart and soul to the world.

By creating legal steps that have some "ease" in them, you've been introduced to complex legal concepts in a down-to-earth, simplified way. By infusing spirituality into the conversation, seeing legal steps aligned with business principles and chakras, I now hope that you feel far more comfortable taking actions now to get legally covered.

You now know 7 easy legal steps...that are also good for your soul.

Going forward, there are 3 things I want for you:

3 Things I Want for You

1. **I want you to feel comfortable holding firm boundaries** so you can feel confident and empowered as a business owner. I want you to stop giving refunds when you don't want to do so, and no longer give away endless time, knowledge and expertise completely for free because you're afraid to ask for payment from clients.

2. **I want you to feel ease in using legal documents**, like do-it-yourself legal templates, creating corporate entities like an LLC or S-Corp, and filing for Trademark protection so you can avoid legal troubles, stressful headaches, and nail-biting distress in your business.

3. **I want you to be aware how the law supports you energetically** so you have greater safety, courage and confidence to go out and create exactly what you want.

And on a personal note, remember that when you approach your work with heartfelt service, you attract people who want to work with you in a heartfelt way. Love attracts loving clients. Courage attracts courageous clients. Your ability to be human, flawed, and vulnerable attracts clients and friends and coaches who are okay with you being human, flawed, and vulnerable, so don't be afraid to let your authentic self be visible in your work.

Although it was scary for me to integrate the chakras into my work and to become a lawyer whose brand is all about Legal Love™, it's been life-changing for me – and for my clients.

I still have a huge amount of respect for lawyers and the law firm in which I was trained, and I didn't want in any way to be perceived as harming lawyers, not taking the profession seriously, or not giving the proper amount of respect to the law by stepping outside of the box and using plain English in legal templates, color in legal documents, and coaching principles when easing legal worries.

But, I've found that infusing a little more Legal Love™ into the law, you as a business owner who may not have felt comfortable taking legal steps to protect yourself now can feel safe to do so – and that's the whole reason why I do the work that I do.

Going forward, know that legal steps help you to create the future of your business so you can express what's in your heart and soul. Rise up to a new level in your business and courageously take the right legal steps to help you get there faster, knowing that lawyers and legal documents are there to fully support you and to have your back.

Congratulations!

Congratulations on now knowing the 7 legal steps to move from stuck and scared of the law to confident and empowered as a business owner. You can feel full of confidence to go forward and create whatever you want— because you know how to get legally covered to feel safe and secure as a business owner and build the business of your wildest dreams.

Legal Love™ Bonus Content

G et a head start in getting legally covered and applying some of the soul-centered principles to your business by grabbing each of free downloads mentioned in the Legal Love™ Bonus Content sections at the end of each chapter. They're worth over $1,300 – and they're my gift to you!

Chapter 1.
Website Disclaimer. Clarity. Root Chakra.
"6 Key Sections that Should Be in Every Website Disclaimer"
Free download at lisafraley.com/disclaimerkeysections ($197 value)

Chapter 2.
Client Agreement. Boundaries. Sacral Chakra.
"5 Critical Components of Every Client Agreement"
Free download at lisafraley.com/clientagreementcriticalcomponents
($197 value)

Chapter 3.
Business Registration and Taxes. Confidence. Solar Plexus Chakra.
"Top 10 Questions to Ask When Hiring an Accountant"
Free download at lisafraley.com/accountant ($197 value)

Chapter 4.
Website Terms & Conditions and Privacy Policy.
Courage. Heart Chakra.

"Website Terms & Conditions Prep Sheet"
Free download at lisafraley.com/websitetermsprepsheet. ($197 value)

Chapter 5.

Terms of Use for Online Programs & Products.
Communication. Throat Chakra.

"Cease and Desist Letter" template.
Free download at lisafraley.com/diyceaseanddesistletter
($197 value - Use code CEASE)

Chapter 6.

LLCs and S-Corps. Intuition. Third Eye Chakra.

"10 Questions to Ask When Hiring an Attorney"
Free download at lisafraley.com/attorneyquestions ($197 value)

Chapter 7.

Trademark. Leadership. Crown Chakra.

"How Do You Know What's Trademark-Worthy?" Assessment.
Free download at lisafraley.com/diytrademarkassessment ($147 value -
Use code WORTHY)

Acknowledgments

I t is next to impossible to name and thank every beautiful soul who has encouraged and nurtured me along the way, but I would be remiss if I didn't shower some #legallove on a number of people who have played key roles in my journey to become an author.

THANK YOU to my coaches and mentors for holding the vision and believing in me ... sometimes more than I have believed in myself:

- **Mike Iamele** for teaching me about the intelligence of apple tree who devotes its energy to creating apples rather than worrying about who comes along to enjoy them; for honoring me with your advice and wisdom as a published author, sacred branding expert, business coach, public relations professional, and supportive friend – and for graciously writing the Foreward to this book.

- **Carey Peters & Stacey Morgenstern** for seeing an eager, budding health coach and teaching me how to courageously "step into my spotlight" as a multi-6-figure entrepreneur.

- **Marie Forleo** for creating B-School and its supportive community which allowed me to birth my online legal courses and templates, connect with magical clients, hire team members and make dear friends.

- **Mike Koenigs** and **Ed Rush** for teaching me the power of online publishing which enabled me to become a #1 Best Selling Author on Amazon in multiple categories.

- **Joshua Rosenthal** and the **Institute for Integrative Nutrition** for giving me the tools to free myself from sugar addiction, and creating a worldwide network of like-minded health coaches passionately devoted to causing a ripple effect by helping clients stop eating junk and start drinking smoothies.

- **Thomas Leonard,** may he rest in peace, and **CoachU** for introducing the world and me to life coaching, and providing me with 3 years of coach training back in 2003 that I didn't know what to do with until 2012 when it dawned on me that I could bring coaching principles into a legal context.

- **Robyn McKay** for marrying psychology and fashion and helping me embrace both my inner "smart girl" and external "blonde bombshell."

- **Stacy Nelson** for raising my marketing simply by drawing a colorful mind-map of my business as a red designer handbag and calling me the "Kate Spade of lawyers" back in 2012.

- **Gina Gomez** for showing me it's possible to tout Law of Attraction principles alongside savvy and effective business coaching strategies when working with clients.

- **Priscilla Stephan** for knowing (before I did!) that I would publish a book about my belief in the "and" over the "or" and the feminine and the masculine sides to the law.

- **Lana Shlafer** for helping me create greater "ease" in allowing myself to more fully receive the income and goodness that the Universe had in store for me.

- **Ixchel Stella** for your bi-weekly healing sessions - and eternal patience – to help me work through past life regressions, persistent karmic contracts, and lingering energy blocks.

- **Belinda Ginter** for your unique blend of emotional kinesiology and intuition combined with your heart-centered observations that illuminated and shifted some age-old beliefs.

- **Keri Nola** for inspiring me as a licensed mental health professional who dares to tap into your spiritual side, and as a soul sister who grounds, supports and truly sees me.

- **Alexis Saloutos** for teaching me everything I know about clearing chakra blocks through your stellar Chakredy® system, and for your friendship which feeds my heart and soul.

- **Sylvaine Hughson** for showering me with wonderful friendship through the past few years of uncomfortable stretching and expanding in business and in life, and for witnessing the letting go and letting in of ideas and beliefs about my past, present and future.

- **Dr. Christiane Northrup** for the personal encouragement to find my courage to express my non-traditional views about a traditional profession (something she knows a bit about.)

THANK YOU to the lawyers who have invited me into your fold - then and now - to share in your passion and knowledge about how to be a good attorney – both "inside the box" and "out of the box."

- **Marty Baxter, Catherine Ballard, Jim Flynn and Bette Squeglia,** as current and retired partners of Bricker & Eckler LLP who invested the time to personally mentor, deeply encourage, and graciously teach me the complexities of health care law in such a highly-regarded law firm.

- **Genavieve Shingle Jaffe** for being my legal Gemini twin, joint venture partner, and swanky photo shoot cohort for our team-taught "Damsel goes bare" online legal course – and for becoming a dear friend.

THANK YOU to some of my strongest supporters and the brightest lights in my life, my **Maine Rockstar Mastermind Sisters** who've watched me go from scared to soaring:

- **Carrie Montgomery** for dressing me up, making me feel pretty, and helping me fight my visibility demons as I showed up on video to show down my fears.

- **Christina Neuner** for declaring me a "spiritual lawyer" the second you met me and holding the grandest visions of me standing on big stages alongside big superstars.

- **Kate Northrup** for being a natural wayshower as a Hay House author and Mastermind sister holding the lantern for me – and for so many others - without overpowering or diminishing the "origin" of our own bright lights.

- **Amber Lilyestrom** for bringing your heartfelt, Soul-Centered CEO® inspiration to all that you do and for inspiring me through the way you live your life out loud with poise and panache.

- **Laura Thompson Brady** for blessing everyone you meet, including me, with your gifts of song, spirit, sound healing and sisterhood as a true Mama on a Mission®.

- **Licia Morelli** for astutely encouraging me to write this book solely for myself as if no one was watching and whose sage writing advice reflects the acclaimed children's author you are.

- **Erin Melito** for your devotion to rigorous training and rock-solid abs combined with your heart of gold and super-cute hairdo showing me that a woman can be both fierce and feminine at once.

- **Kelsey Abbott** for your aim in athletics and in life to find "inconspicuously awesome" moments to stop and smell the roses on a daily basis.

THANK YOU to my team of uber-talented, multi-dimensional creatives for your never-ending patience and grace as my random scribbles and journal entries were turned into this book:

- **Laura Belgray** for your unmatched copywriting skills which unfurled "get legally covered so you can go bare" as the name of my flagship legal course, and for your love of gelato which gave me a perfect excuse to attend your writing workshop in a 12th century castle surrounded by lemon trees and olive groves in Cinqueterre, Italy.

- **Anjanette Fennell** for your expertise as a professional literary coach and agent combined with your caring coaching skills that coaxed the ideas out of my mind and onto the paper over 6 months, chapter by chapter, giving me the freedom and safety to write this book directly from my heart.

- **Sarah Barbour** for your thorough copy editing through Aeroplane Media as you "flew in" and gracefully massaged my verbosity, which is definitely an art form and not an exact science.

- **Michelle Schweitzer** for your proofreading proficiency in catching and correcting my grammatical errors, yet, honoring my conversational tone that is fully and intentionally grammatically incorrect.

- **Cassi Goozen** for your creative graphic designs and colorful expressions that have given beautiful dimension to my book cover, my business and my brand.

- **Laura Sprinkle** for your endurance as my website developer for "hurrying up and waiting" during the creation of my new site so it could be divinely timed with the publication of this book.

- **Heather Jernigan**, my Creative Marketing Director, my Robin to my Batman, who is the one person who tirelessly works behind the scenes to make "wearing of the crown" look so easy, for your multi-talented, creative, leadership and organizational skills to plan and prepare the marketing and messaging of our #legallove mission; for your generosity, groundedness and grace as we've toiled through this book, website and business together; and for simultaneously and pricelessly gifting me with your true-blue friendship as my best biz confidante, for which I am forever grateful.

THANK YOU to my loving family who accepts my faults, embraces my talents, endures my idiosyncrasies, and makes me proud to be one among you:

- **Sandy Sullivan, Jim Fraley, Blair Fraley, Tyler Fraley, Shelley Fraley, Matt Fraley, Katrina Fraley, Alex Fraley, Lance Fraley, Larz Fraley, Maki Fraley, Kelli Morningstar,** and **Mark Morningstar,** for welcoming me as a "Fraley" with your warmth and kindness twelve years ago, for inviting me into your Pennsylvania family and into your homes, for sharing Scott with me, and for loving me up as my parents-in-law, siblings-in-law, nieces and nephews.

- **Bart Patton, Jessica Patton, Kaitlyn Patton and Lindsay Patton,** for being so openly loving to Scott, Meghan and me whether a day or a year has passed since we've been together, for letting me be your "Aunt LiLi", and for being such thoughtful and kind human beings.

- **Meghan Fraley,** my beautiful step-daughter, for making room in your heart for a second "mama" in your life, for blessing me with your energy and fun-loving spirit, for teaching me German phrases since you were 10 years old, and for letting me love you.

- **Ellen Hanger,** my wonderful paternal grandmother, for holding the vision and defiantly declaring that since you couldn't become a doctor (like your father) at a time when women were relegated to the home, you would ensure that your children/grandchildren had the means to be educated to achieve our dreams.

- **Robert J. Hanger,** my treasured paternal grandfather, for funding my legal education - just as my grandmother had wanted – and for giving me permission to leave the practice of law for a while, only to return years later to help others in a way that brings me so much joy and satisfaction.

- **Nancy Hanger**, my inspiring mother, for demonstrating what it means to be a strong, smart woman, for modeling to me how to "do my best" and excel in school, for supporting my life and business choices, for honoring my decades of crazy eating habits (and too many diets to count!), and for loving me unconditionally.

- **Bill Hanger**, my loving father, for raising me to believe that I could grow up to be "anything I want" so long as I am making a difference in the world, for teaching me how to bravely stand up for others who don't have a voice, for teaching me to be inclusive of all people, and for being my champion.

- **Jill Patton**, my precious sister, for accepting my apology for not playing more Barbies with you when we were girls, for evolving into my closest friend who has supported me through happiness, healing and heartbreaks, for always making me (and everyone else we know) feel like I am the most important person in the world, and for always dropping everything to listen and love me.

- **Scott Fraley**, my beloved husband, for being the most courageous man I know, for believing in me that I could actually build a business and write this (endless!) book, for being my superhero and my heart's anchor and my happy place, for sacrificing weekend hikes and movie nights so I could hole up in my office and work, for inspiring me with your past accomplishments, accolades and adventures, for letting me know how loved I am multiple times a day every single day, and for the beautiful gift of sharing your life with me.

And, finally, with a full heart and endless gratitude...

THANK YOU to my clients and readers who are journeying with me for the important, life-changing work you are doing in this world, for your vision and determination to share your gifts "out of the box", and for walking beside me as I share these easy legal steps with you to help you honor and protect that which you are working so hard to build.

About the Author

Photography ©Amber Lilyestrom

Lisa Fraley, JD, is an acclaimed attorney, Legal Coach®, speaker, and sought-after expert on small business law. With her unique blend of coaching, legal expertise, and spirituality, Lisa has supported thousands of heart-centered entrepreneurs and small business owners to protect themselves, their businesses and their brands.

From sharing international stages with thought leaders like Kris Carr and Gabrielle Bernstein to being featured on hundreds of podcasts, webinars, radio shows and bonus calls, Lisa has made it her mission to help every single coach, entrepreneur and small business owner understand that the law can be accessible, empowering, loving - and even spiritual. When she's not saving the world with Legal Love™ one contract at a time, Lisa enjoys hiking, running, traveling and eating gluten-free cupcakes with her husband Scott.

lisafraley.com

Endnotes

1 Coach U was founded by Thomas Leonard, who is known as the "father of life coaching," and who counts Marie Forleo and Cheryl Richardson as Coach U grads. For more information about Coach U, see www.coachu-hq.com

2 I also referred them to other attorneys to assist with their specific legal situations, as needed.

3 This definition of "boundary" is derived from the definition found in Merriam-Webster's Dictionary online. www.merriam-webster.com/dictionary/boundary.

4 This statistic was obtained from the *American Journal of Physiology.* Am J Physiol. 1999 Nov; 277 (5 Pt 1): G922-8.

5 To summarize, the Mayo Clinic Staff reports in a blog post titled "Germs: Understand and protect against bacteria, viruses and infection" that inside our gut, there are both "good bacteria" called probiotics which are a key part of the immune system and whose role it is to fight off the "bad bacteria" in the gut flora which can produce toxins that damage cells, cause illness, and contribute to many serious health issues, ranging from serious autoimmune diseases to urinary tract infections to strep throat. www.mayoclinic.org/germs/art-20045289.

6 The idea of the "second brain" is reported by Scientific American on their website in an article titled "Think Twice: How the Gut's 'Second Brain' Influences Mood and Well-Being." www.scientificamerican.com/article/gut-second-brain. Additionally, the enteric nervous system is defined by

Dr. John B. Furness, University of Melbourne, Australia as the "intrinsic nervous system of the gastrointestinal tract". www.scholarpedia.org/article/Enteric_nervous_system. The enteric nervous system is a mesh-like neurological network that runs through the sheaths of the linings of the esophagus, stomach, small intestine and colon where nerves send and transmit neurological impulses and use 30 neurotransmitters such as dopamine, norepinephrine and serotonin—the same ones that our brain uses—to impact mood. Since "95% of serotonin is found in the bowels", that's a clear indication that our gut plays an important role in how we feel on a daily basis. www.scientificamerican.com/article/gut-second-brain. Our gut literally is impacting our mood.

[7]   Neuro-linguistic programming (NLP) is defined as a "set of rules and techniques proposed for modifying behavior in achieving self-improvement, self-management, and more effective interpersonal communications. Its basic premise is that, to achieve any kind of success, one must create rich imagery of the goal, and must imitate (model) and internalize the appropriate behavioral patterns. Its name is derived from how senses filter and process experience before storing it in brain (neuro), how one uses words and symbols to create mental pictures (linguistic), and how desired habits and attitudes become ingrained (programming)." www.businessdictionary.com/definition/neuro-linguistic-programming-NLP.html.

[8]   More information about "courage" being derived from the word "heart" may be found in the Online Etymology Dictionary under the definition of "Courage." etymonline.com/index.php?allowed_in_frame=0&search=courage.

[9]   Lesson 293 from *A Course in Miracles©*: Combined Volume is from the 3rd Edition, published in 2007, by the Foundation for Inner Peace, P.O. Box 598, Mill Valley, CA 94942-0598, www.acim.org and info@acim.org; Williamson, Marianne (2009). *A Return to Love: Reflections on the Principles of "A Course in Miracles"* (HarperCollins); Bernstein, Gabrielle. (2014) *Miracles Now: 108 Life-Changing Tools for Less Stress, More Flow, and Finding Your True Purpose* (Hay House Inc.); 1 John 4:18, The Holy

Bible, New International Version (NIV)(1984) (Grand Rapids: Zondervan Publishing House.)

[10]   1 John 4:18, The Holy Bible, New International Version (NIV)(1984) (Grand Rapids: Zondervan Publishing House.)

[11]   At least one state in the US (California) requires a Privacy Policy. The California Online Privacy Protection Act (CalOPPA) requires any operator of a commercial website to conspicuously post a Privacy Policy on a website if you are collecting personally identifiable information from California residents. The Online Privacy Protection Act of 2003, Cal. Bus. & Prof. Code §§ 22575-22579 (2004). In addition, the Child Online Privacy Protection Act (COPPA) requires that website operators comply with legal requirements that protect the privacy and vulnerability of children. European countries also have strict privacy laws. The law can change at any time so other states or countries may also tighten their requirements in the future. Be sure to speak with a local attorney to assist you.

[12]   This quote is derived from St. Augustine in his Letter 211 (c. 424) that contains the phrase "*Cum dilectione hominium et odio vitorum*", which translates roughly to "With love for mankind and hatred of sins." Through the years, the phrase has become more commonly said as "hate the sin and not the sinner" or "love the sinner but hate the sin."

[13]   I took many political philosophy, jurisprudence, and comparative religion courses in college and law school to try to discover a logical argument to negate that "no belief is absolute." Beliefs may be absolute on a personal level, but I have not found proof that there is absolutism universally, especially as a lawyer who is trained to be able to argue two sides to any position. Should you feel otherwise, I am open to hearing opposing arguments, provided they are expressed in a loving, friendly manner.

[14]   I stated that we are free to "think and believe what we wish", but I deliberately did not say that we also are free to "ACT as we wish." Thoughts are not regulated by the United States government - but actions are. For better

and for worse, our country's Forefathers gave us the freedom to think and believe what we wish in our own minds. Fortunately, there are many federal, state, and local laws appropriately forbidding people from taking actions or speaking in ways that tread on others' legal rights and human rights.

15   Technically, there are a few "subjective standard" tests used in law, such as when determining *mens rea* (state of mind) of a defendant in a criminal case, so subjectivity can have a limited place in a courtroom, but it's not widely used outside of those select situations.

16   In US Federal Rules of Evidence, Rule 702. Testimony by Expert Witnesses, it states: "A witness who is qualified as an expert by knowledge, skill, experience, training, or education may testify in the form of an opinion or otherwise if: (a) the expert's scientific, technical, or other specialized knowledge will help the trier of fact to understand the evidence or to determine a fact in issue; (b) the testimony is based on sufficient facts or data; (c) the testimony is the product of reliable principles and methods; and (d) the expert has reliably applied the principles and methods to the facts of the case."

17   In US Federal Rule of Evidence, Rule 701. Opinion Testimony by Lay Witnesses, it states: "If a witness is not testifying as an expert, testimony in the form of an opinion is limited to one that is: (a) rationally based on the witness's perception; (b) helpful to clearly understanding the witness's testimony or to determining a fact in issue; and (c) not based on scientific, technical, or other specialized knowledge within the scope of Rule 702."

18   A simple definition for "natural law" is "a principle or body of laws considered as derived from nature, right reason, or religion and as ethically binding in human society." www.dictionary.com/browse/natural-law

19   Generally speaking, clairvoyance is "(from French clair meaning "clear" and voyance meaning "vision") [and] is the alleged ability to gain information about an object, person, location or physical event through extrasensory perception. Any person who is claimed to have some such ability is said accordingly to be a clairvoyant ("one who sees

clearly").” Likewise, clairaudience, clairsentience and claircognizance rely on information gained by auditory, sensations or internal knowledge, respectively. www.en.wikipedia.org/wiki/Clairvoyance

[20]   This statistic was derived from a 2015 survey conducted by the Minority Corporate Council Association and Vault.com Inc. as outlined in the “Vault/MCAA Law Firm Diversity Student Report”. www.mcca.com/index.cfm?fuseaction=page.viewpage&pageid=2624

[21]   Bloomberg reported in an article “The Best Law Schools Are Attracting Fewer Students” that fewer students are applying to law schools and some top law schools are reducing the size of law school classes. www.bloomberg.com/news/articles/2016-01-26/the-best-law-schools-are-attracting-fewer-students

[22]   This book is focused on the corporate entities most used by solo business owners. However, if you wish to form an LLC with more than just one owner, you would create a multi-member LLC, and by default, your LLC will be treated as a partnership for tax purposes, unless you elect to be taxed as an S-Corp. Talk with an attorney and accountant if you wish to set up a multi-member LLC, as there are additional considerations.

[23]   A C-Corporation is not generally used by small business owners. It's a corporate entity that is taxed separately from its owners so the company pays taxes AND the shareholders (owners) pay taxes on the company's income. If you're the owner, this means you pay taxes at two levels—both on the personal level and the corporate level. This is called “double taxation.” For larger corporations, despite the “double taxation” requirement, there are many advantages to being a C-Corp, but for solopreneurs without plans for different classes of stock or multiple owners or investors, C-Corporations aren't as ideal.

[24]   The original case was tried in federal district court in the state of New York as Kelly-Brown et al. v. Winfrey et al., US District Court (S.D. New York,), No. 1:11-cv-07875. After a long legal process, in September 2016, the decision was upheld on appeal in favor of Oprah by the Second Circuit Court in Kelly-Brown et al. v. Winfrey et al., 2nd US Circuit Court of Appeals, No. 15-697.